New World of Wonders

AMERICA

T' AMSTERDAM
By Jacob van Meurs, *Plaetsnyder en Boeckverkooper op de Keysers graft in de Stadt Meurs. 1671.*

New World of Wonders

European Images of the Americas
1492–1700

Edited by Rachel Doggett

with Monique Hulvey and Julie Ainsworth

The Folger Shakespeare Library
Washington, D.C.
1992

Distributed by
University of Washington Press
Seattle and London

This volume has been published in conjunction with the exhibition *New World of Wonders: European Images of the Americas, 1492–1700*, on display at the Folger Library, Washington, D.C., from October 8, 1992, to March 6, 1993.

The exhibition and publication have been funded in part by a generous grant from the National Endowment for the Humanities.

Publication Director: Janet Alexander Griffin, Director of Museum and Public Programs
Editorial and Production Coordinator: Jane E. Bissonnette
Edited, designed, and produced by Marquand Books, Inc., Seattle

Printed in the United States

Distributed by University of Washington Press

Library of Congress Cataloging-in-Publication Data

New world of wonders : European images of the Americas, 1492–1700 / edited by Rachel
    Doggett, with Monique Hulvey and Julie Ainsworth.
        p.   cm.
      Published in conjunction with an exhibition at the Folger Shakespeare Library, Oct. 8,
    1992–Mar. 6, 1993.
        Includes bibliographical references and index.
        ISBN 0-295-97247-5
        1. America—History—To 1810—Pictorial works—Exhibitions. 2. America in art—
    Exhibitions. 3. Indians—Pictorial works—Exhibitions. 4. Natural history—America—
    Pictorial works—Exhibitions. I. Doggett, Rachel. II. Hulvey, Monique. III. Ainsworth,
    Julie. IV. Folger Shakespeare Library.
    E18.82.N48   1992
    973.1'074753—dc20   92-28277

Cover: Ulisse Aldrovandi, *Ornithologiae* (cat. no. 42), and Giovanni Battista Ramusio, *Delle Navigationi et Viaggi* (cat. no. 2).
Frontispiece: Arnoldus Montanus, *De Nieuwe en Onbekende Weereld* (cat. no. 84).

Photographs by Julie Ainsworth except as follows: pp. 13, 93, Houghton Library, Harvard University; p. 24, New York Public Library; p. 26, Biblioteca Trivulziana, Milan; p. 27, Bayerische Staatsbibliothek, Munich; p. 28, Museo de Grão Vasco, Viseu; p. 29, National Museum of Denmark; pp. 54–57, the British Museum; p. 69, cat. no. 29, William C. Sturtevant; p. 69, cat. nos. 30–31, National Museum of Natural History, Smithsonian Institution; p. 84, Dumbarton Oaks, Washington, D.C.; pp. 99–104, Peter Willi, Paris; pp. 116, 140, 142–143, 146–147, Courtauld Institute of Art, London.

Editor's note: Original spellings have been retained in quotations except for i-j and u-v, which have been altered to conform to modern usage.

Contents

Introduction

In George Chapman's *The Memorable Maske*, performed in London in 1613 during celebrations for the marriage of Princess Elizabeth to the Elector Palatine, the chief masquers appeared in Indian habits richly embroidered with golden suns. "On their heads [were] high sprig'd-feathers. . . . Their legges were adorn'd, with close long white silke-stockings. . . . And over these (being on horse backe) they drew greaves or buskins embrodered with gould, & enterlac't with rewes of fethers; Altogether estrangfull, and *Indian* like." Chapman's masquers were probably not intended to be accurate representations of Indians, but his description of them and their land of "Virginia" reminds us that more than 100 years after 1492, New World peoples and customs were little understood in the Old World: they were still "Altogether estrangfull." For the vast majority of Europeans it was not easy to imagine and visualize a new land and a way of life that was so completely different from their own and that was not accounted for in human history as they knew it.

How did most Europeans begin to form their images of this New World—not only of the people but also of the flora, fauna, and rich resources of the land? Beginning with Columbus, people could read printed accounts by those who had traveled to the New World or by authors like Peter Martyr, Giovanni Battista Ramusio, and Richard Hakluyt who collected and published the accounts of others. Even those who could not read would have heard reports of the new discoveries. But also, again beginning with Columbus, New World peoples, artifacts, plant and animal specimens, gold, and silver were taken back to Europe. During the 16th and 17th centuries the average European citizen had numerous opportunities to experience aspects of the New World through this physical evidence.

Artifacts and specimens brought back, at first, as proof of an expedition's success were soon sought after by collectors. Beginning in the 16th century, there was an unprecedented interest in assembling curios and in amassing information about the customs, dress, and beliefs of other cultures. Although this fascination with other cultures may initially have sprung from a desire to be entertained and was often characterized by an emphasis on the bizarre, by the 17th century people demonstrated a serious desire to study and understand the objects and information collected. This was the age of the wonder cabinet or cabinet of curiosities, when "wonder" was celebrated. For early modern Europeans, as for us, wonder is often the first step toward study and learning.

This exhibition and accompanying catalogue draw on the Folger Library's incomparable collections of 16th- and 17th-century books and engravings to illustrate how some of Europe's ideas about the New World developed. Although many of the cabinets of curiosities put together by private collectors were available only to a limited number of learned individuals, some—like Ulisse Aldrovandi's in Bologna—were accessible to the public. New World plants were grown in botanic gardens, such as those associated with the universities at Padua and Leiden. Animals appeared in game parks and as skinned and sometimes stuffed specimens in private collections, as well as in books and paintings. Examples of New World dress, and even its wearers, were brought back by explorers and displayed, sometimes on board ship or at dockside, to any who would come to see them.

New World of Wonders documents the presence of New World peoples in Europe and some reactions to them. It also explores the impact of the work of artists, such as John White, who traveled to the New World and drew what they saw there. It examines the engravings of those who copied from White as well as from other sources and explains how inaccuracies occurred. And it recreates a portion of a wonder cabinet using artifacts that have been part of the cabinet of the Bibliothèque Sainte-Geneviève in Paris since the 17th century.

In addition to documenting some of the ways in which the New World was on display, the exhibition and catalogue illustrate the manner in which the New World was depicted or represented not only by writers, artists, and engravers but also by actors on the stage and in public festivities such as royal entries. Some of the elaborate masques performed at the Stuart court incorporated "Indians" or New World settings, with costumes and sets designed by Inigo Jones.

The exhibition and catalogue demonstrate some of the confusions that occur when cultures collide. In spite of the people, artifacts, and specimens that could be seen fairly widely, for many Europeans a few selected images, primarily the feathers and gold emphasized by Chapman, came to signify "Indians" and "America." Much of what could be seen was presented haphazardly and without a context in which it could be understood. And since great emphasis was given to the strangest and most exotic details, those are the ones that appear to have taken root in the popular imagination, making their way into drama and public pageantry and, ultimately, into symbolic depictions of America as the fourth continent. Difference attracts us, and all the things that made America different from Europe constituted the predominant European vision of the New World. This brief survey of that developing vision may enlighten us about the ways in which we, even today, encounter and interpret cultures other than our own.

A large number of people have had a hand in making this exhibition and catalogue possible. Above all, thanks must go to the National Endowment for the Humanities for both a planning grant and a very generous implementation grant in support of the project. We are also very grateful to His Grace, the duke of Devonshire, the Trustees of the Chatsworth Settlement, and to Peter Day, keeper of the Chatsworth collections, for the loan of five marvelous Inigo Jones drawings. Françoise Zehnacker, keeper of the cabinet, and Geneviève Boisard, director of the Bibliothèque Sainte-Geneviève, Paris, were very helpful in arranging the loan of their New World treasures. Donald J. Ortner, chairman of the Department of Anthropology of the National Museum of Natural History, Smithsonian Institution, made it possible for us to display several objects of gold and featherwork from their collections.

Throughout the planning of the exhibition, four scholarly consultants gave generously of their time and expertise and have contributed essays to this catalogue: Dr. Steven Mullaney of the Department of English, University of Michigan; Dr. William Sturtevant of the Department of Anthropology, National Museum of Natural History; Dr. Alden T. Vaughan of the Department of History, Columbia University; and Dr. Virginia Mason Vaughan of the Department of English, Clark University.

On the library's own staff, Peggy O'Brien, head of the Education Department, deserves special thanks for her role in planning a workshop for teachers and an educational packet for the use of students, librarians, and teachers. Janet Griffin, director of Museum and Public Programs, has put together an exciting array of programs to accompany and enhance the exhibition and, with her assistant, Jane Bissonnette, has played a major role behind the scenes in various stages of the production of the exhibition and the catalogue. Frank Mowery, head of Conservation, and Julia Stevenson, senior paper conservator, worked closely with Barbara Charles and other members of the firm of Staples and Charles on the design and mounting of the exhibition.

An exhibition such as this enables the public to enjoy and learn from the Folger Library's collections and to use these scholarly resources to illuminate aspects of our history and culture that have not been fully understood. Among the privileges of the curator's role are exploring the collections and assembling materials both to enlighten and entertain our visitors. Monique Hulvey, senior cataloger, and Julie Ainsworth, head of the Photography Department, spent many hours on research and book selection and contributed beyond the scope of their usual specialities in preparing this publication. We hope that as you view the exhibition, or read the catalogue, you too will derive some sense of the excitement and wonder experienced by the Old World in its early encounters with the New.

Rachel Doggett
Andrew W. Mellon Curator of Books

An American tree with three trunks from Giovanni Battista Ramusio,
Delle Navigationi Et Viaggi (Venice, 1554–1559).

People of Wonder

England Encounters the New World's Natives

Alden T. Vaughan

Early European accounts of America often described it as "wonderful," using the word in its original sense: full of wonder or awe. That quality was not necessarily good or desirable—terrors could be awesome, too—but the new-found land was eye-opening and breathtaking in either case, for it was simultaneously grand and forbidding. Europeans of all nationalities agreed that America was truly wonderful because it seemed so different from their world. To call it a New World—even before anyone labeled it America or understood that it was separate from Asia—was to suggest much more than recent discovery. The Western hemisphere bombarded the senses with new sights, sounds, and smells; it provoked new questions, offered new evidence, and demanded new conclusions about the earth and its inhabitants.

The land itself excited Europe's fancy. Whether an explorer encountered the lush forest and dank climate of the tropics or the barren tundra and frigid air of the northern latitudes, America's environment—at its extremes, at least—differed drastically from Italy's or Spain's or England's. And as Europeans pushed farther and farther into the interior of the two continents, they encountered topographical wonders—majestic mountains, seemingly bottomless ravines, lakes the size of small oceans. Europe paled by comparison, or so the explorers contended. On Columbus's first transatlantic voyage, he declared that Hispaniola (the island now shared by Haiti and the Dominican Republic) "is a wonder," with "many large harbours finer than any I know in Christian lands"; the island itself

he judged to be "greater in circumference than the whole of Spain"; the places he visited were "the most fertile and temperate . . . and good in the whole world."[1] The Admiral, to be sure, was in a mood to exaggerate, but those who came after him were often as hyperbolic. New World geography was genuinely amazing.

More astounding than the New World's topographical wonders, because more plentiful, were many of its strange trees, flowers, grasses, and vegetables. Again Columbus: "[A]ll these trees are as different from ours as day from night and so are the fruit and plants and . . . everything else."[2] America's unique flora would soon have European names (corruptions, usually, of native nomenclature): maize, potatoes, yams, beans of many kinds, squashes, pumpkins, pineapples, rubber, tobacco. European explorers were also surprised by the absence in America of many species that the Old World took for granted. How could a whole hemisphere not have wheat or barley or rice or oats? How could it not have sugar or olives or bananas? The differences in nature's bounty between the Old World and the New were so great that the eventual exchange of samples and seeds would revolutionize food production around the globe.[3]

Overshadowing the wonder of the New World's flora was the still more dramatic novelty of its fauna. Europeans could scarcely imagine life without horses, cattle, sheep, goats, and pigs; America had none of them. Even the destructive but ubiquitous rat was nowhere to be found. The complete absence of such creatures, both good and bad, from the New

11

World suggested to some observers a separate creation—a heretical notion to orthodox Christians but tempting nonetheless. How else could one explain the lack of animals so essential to European husbandry and the presence, instead, of such exotic creatures as armadillos, anteaters, tree sloths, iguanas, electric eels, vampire bats, hummingbirds, and flying squirrels? That these animals could not be harnessed to human needs only added to the mysterious character of the Americas and to European suspicions that the newly discovered lands were—despite their impressive geography and useful plants—a lesser part of God's creation, lands to be conquered and cultivated for Europe's benefit.

Coincident with exploration and conquest was collection. Columbus carried back to Spain from his first voyage a wide variety of American wonders, partly as proof that he had indeed reached the other side of the world and partly as evidence of its marvels. For each subsequent voyage by Columbus and his many successors, collecting specimens was an essential part of the mission. To some extent Europe's craving for New World samples was scientific: learned men wanted to know as much as possible about the American environment. Much of the interest, however, was simple curiosity about New World specimens, whether animal, vegetable, or mineral. The menagerie at the Tower of London, for example, housed a fabulous assortment of American wildlife—eagles, raccoons, porcupines, flying squirrels, and the like. On the Continent, especially, collectors in several nations constructed "wonder cabinets" or even whole rooms to display exotic objects (especially American), both natural and man-made, from hatchets to headdresses, from costumes to canoes, from snowshoes to stuffed animals. European horticulturists, meanwhile, fashioned gardens with separate sections for plants from the four continents, with one section devoted to rare American species.

America's human inhabitants excited the most interest of all. Here again, Columbus was not only the first to describe them but the first

Armadillo from Juan Eusebio Nieremberg, *Historia Naturae Maxime Peregrinae* (Antwerp, 1635).

to take some back to Europe. Shortly after his initial landfall in the Bahamas, Columbus recorded his impressions of the natives' appearance, customs, and character, emphasizing the features that distinguished them from Europeans—their nakedness, body paint, hairstyles, and absence (he thought) of religion. He made similar observations at the other islands he visited, and en route back to Spain he collated his findings in a long description of the natives he had encountered. With its publication, Europeans could read about the people on the other side of the globe.

Some Europeans could actually see Indians. At each island Columbus obtained a few natives—volunteers or, more often, captives. He took several to Spain in 1493; a year later the cargo from his second voyage included about 600 natives, all captives. Two hundred or so died at sea; half the remainder were ill by the time they reached port, and most of Columbus's New World captives soon succumbed to European diseases. That did not end Europe's fascination with coerced American envoys. Indians continued to arrive in irregular but substantial numbers throughout the rest of the 15th century and long after, often as slaves but often too as unwilling showpieces for European curiosity. An Indian on display, Shakespeare would observe in *The Tempest*, could earn its owner a small fortune. And if the supply of real Indians did not satisfy Europe's entertainment needs—for pageants, parades, and other festivities—ersatz natives could readily be created by adorning

The museum of the Danish collector Ole Worm as illustrated on the engraved title page to his *Museum Wormianum* (Leiden, 1655; reproduced with the permission of the Houghton Library, Harvard University).

Old World denizens in feathers and paint. Such masquerading was done on a grand scale at the pageant for France's Henri II at Rouen in 1550, where hundreds of pseudo-Indians and some real Indians temporarily inhabited a mock Indian village. On a much smaller scale, Renaissance stage performances increasingly included one or more "Indians" as representatives of the new world of wonders.

English people in the Tudor era lagged noticeably behind other Europeans in learning about the Americas. For nearly a century, English interest in the New World was surprisingly tangential, more a matter of curiosity than of conquest and based primarily on foreign rather than on English observations. Although England

shared the general European fascination with America, only in the last quarter of the 16th century did she become actively involved in the exploration and conquest of the land and its peoples. Thereafter, England's image of American natives reflected uniquely English experiences and expectations.

Variations in national outlooks existed from the outset, of course. The Spanish, Portuguese, French, Dutch, and English (to name only the major colonizing peoples) had different imperial careers and brought disparate assumptions to their encounters with American natives. Despite those differences and the intense international rivalries that embroiled Europe in almost constant diplomatic and military struggle, the imperial powers shared many fundamental ideas, both secular and religious, about the New World. They agreed, for example, on the intrinsic superiority of European religious beliefs and structures, forms of government and law, concepts of property and privacy, customs of clothing, feeding, and manners. Europeans of every nationality assumed that wherever Indian culture strayed from European norms—which it usually did—Indian ways were savage, uncivil, and therefore unacceptable. European cultures, their adherents insisted, were right; Indian cultures were wrong. Accordingly, Europeans expected Indians to embrace Christianity and to adopt, as rapidly as possible, European political, economic, and social customs. But first, Europeans, including the insular English, had to learn, slowly and erratically, just who these strangers were.

Columbus provided the first clues. Homeward bound on the *Niña* in February 1493, he described in a letter to Luis de Santangel, keeper of Queen Isabella's privy purse, the remarkable places and people he had seen. Within a month the letter was printed in Castilian; at least 15 editions followed before the end of the century in Latin, Spanish, Italian, and German, but, significantly, not in English. Some English readers nonetheless may have gotten their first vicarious glimpse of American natives through a foreign edition of Columbus's *Epistola*. "The people . . . which I have found and seen," Columbus reported,

> all go naked, men and women, as their mothers bore them, except that some women cover one place only with the leaf of a plant or with a net of cotton which they make for that purpose. They have no iron or steel or weapons, nor are they capable of using them, although they are well-built people of handsome stature, because they are wondrous timid.[4]

Columbus went on to praise the Indians' generosity, intelligence, ingenuity, and eagerness to accept Christianity. All in all, the natives encountered by Columbus were admirable indeed. They seemed to be innocent and pliable creatures of a new golden land.

But Columbus's letter also mentioned strange people he had heard of but had not seen. Some were born with tails; one island was inhabited only by women; the people of another island had no hair. Most shocking of all, the denizens of an especially notorious island were ferocious, unlike any he had met, and feasted on human flesh. Columbus thus suggested the polarities of European assessments of Indians that would flourish for centuries: handsome or grotesque, timid or fierce, intelligent or obtuse, wholly human or bestial. European perceptions of the Indians would fluctuate between the extremes, and sometimes even fuse the extremes, according to varying circumstances and changing assumptions. Rarely did Europeans recognize the variety, complexity, and intrinsic value of Native American cultures. Most observers from the Old World substituted symbols for understanding, shibboleths for sophisticated descriptions.

The first documented contact between the English and the Indians occurred in about 1502, when Sebastian Cabot (or perhaps a ship sent out by Bristol promoters) brought back "iii men takyn In the Newe ffound Ile land"; two of them survived long enough to demonstrate their adaptability to English ways. On arrival they "were clothid In bestys skynnys and ete Rawe fflesh and spak such spech that noo man cowde undyrstand theym, and In theyr demeanure [were] lyke to bruyt bestis." Two years later, the same reporter saw them "apparaylyd afftyr Inglysh men . . ., which at that tyme I cowde not dyscern ffrom Inglysh men tyll I was lernyd what men they were."[5] The apparent success of this early encounter notwithstanding, English interest in America and its inhabitants remained slight. Not until 1530, apparently, were other Indians brought to England, and not until 1553 did an English publisher issue a book with appreciable attention to America's inhabitants. Nor did English sailors, except close-lipped fishermen, frequent the American coast and thus gain impressions of the Indians to spread at home by word of mouth. In the six decades between Columbus's return and Richard Eden's translation into English of a German tract entitled *A Treatyse of the New India*, England had sparse evidence on which to base its images of American Indians.

Before Eden's translation, Continental publications had to fill the gap for English readers with a hodgepodge of information and misinformation. Such writings generally followed Columbus's lead: a mixture of praise and condemnation of the Indians that rarely distinguished one tribe or region from another. Reports by Spaniards, Portuguese, Italians, and others — mostly in Latin — were undoubtedly read by a small circle of English scholars, priests, and government officials. Similarly, a few curious Englishmen must have listened eagerly to tales by sailors who had been to America on a rare English expedition or who had heard descriptions from Continental seafarers. The quantity or impact of such written and oral reports cannot be judged, but England's scant participation in New World exploration before the last quarter of the 16th century and the paucity of English-language publications concerning the New World before mid-century suggest that the influx and influence were negligible.

Only one early 16th-century book in English gave appreciable attention to American natives, and it was published on the Continent, at Antwerp. A brief treatise with a long title, *Of the newe landes and of ye people founde by the messengers of the Kynge of Portyngale named Emanuel* (c. 1511), it described the natives of "Armenica" in exceptionally dismal terms:

> [T]he people of this lande have no kynge nor lorde nor theyre god[.] But all thinges is commune[.] [T]his people goeth all naked. . . . These folke lyven lyke bestes without any resonablenes and the wymen be also as common[.] And the men hath conversacyon with the wymen . . . who they fyrst mete [even if she] is . . . his syster his mother his daughter or any other kyndred. And the wymen be very hoote and dysposed to lecherdnes. And they ete also on[e] a nother. The man etethe his wyfe his chylderne as we also have seen and they hange also the bodyes or persons fleeshe in the smoke as men do With us swynes fleshe.[6]

Europe's revulsion at, yet fascination with, the natives' sexual and cannibalistic practices is palpable.

Reports of cannibalism were not merely shocking; they implied that Indians who ate human flesh might not themselves be human. Of course Europeans had known of anthropophagi, as they called eaters of human flesh, since the works of Herodotus in the 5th century B.C., but such creatures were almost entirely mythical. Now, suddenly, such people had been found in an otherwise paradisaic part of the world. So prominent did some accounts make the eating of human flesh that the word *cannibal*, from the Carib Indians who presumably practiced the vile custom, gradually replaced the older, more awkward, term for eaters of human flesh. And although reporters, beginning with Columbus, insisted that only some Indians ate humans and that other natives abhorred the practice and its practitioners, many chroniclers described cannibalism as a common trait. Amerigo Vespucci, for example, not only lent his name to the land and its peoples but put his stamp on his namesakes as insatiable anthropophagi. In a widely reprinted letter of 1505, Vespucci wrote:

> I knew a man who was popularly credited to have eaten 300 human bodies. I was once in a certain city . . . where human flesh was hung up near the houses, in the same way as we expose butcher's meat. . . . [T]hey were surprised that we did not eat our enemies, and use their flesh as food, for they say it is excellent.[7]

In a grim stroke of irony, Vespucci may have been eaten by Indians.

Sixteenth-century illustrations reinforced the verbal image of widespread and blatant cannibalism. Especially graphic were the woodcut illustrations in several Continental publications, such as Vespucci's *Mundus Novus* (1503 et seq.), showing Indians eating or curing their human victims. Similarly, a German broadside of 1505 carried a large picture of men, women, and children feasting on human parts; the accompanying text offers the already stereotypical list of presumed Indian shortcomings: naked bodies, common ownership, sexual license, frequent warfare, idolatry, and cannibalism. But illustrations may have been especially potent shapers of European imagery: unlike words, pictures could reach Europe's illiterate masses. The humblest residents of any nation could absorb the same pejorative lesson about the Indians that their

Cannibalism as illustrated in André Thevet, *Les Singularitez de la France Antarctique* (Antwerp, 1558).

more learned neighbors were able to glean from the printed page.

In 1553, 60 years after Columbus's return from America and 50 since the first American natives reached England, the availability of English-language information about the Indians increased dramatically. Partly in response to England's growing interest in foreign markets and partly in celebration of the recent rapprochement with Spain that would culminate in Mary Tudor's marriage to the future Philip II, Richard Eden issued *A Treatyse of the Newe India, with Other New Founde Landes and Ilandes*, his translation of a German work by Sebastian Münster. Münster's picture of American natives varied little from earlier Continental publications; gruesome details abound, especially in descriptions of cannibalism. Yet Münster acknowledged that only a few tribes consumed human flesh, and the other tribes held cannibals in contempt. A similar message emerged two years later when Eden edited another Continental account of America and its natives. *Decades of the Newe Worlde* contained extracts from earlier descriptions of America (1511–1516) by Peter Martyr, an Italian scholar living in Spain, plus selections from several other European accounts.

In the preface to the volume, Eden praised Spain for "mercyfull warres ageynst these naked people," who benefited from the conquest more than their conquerors did. Spain, he contended, took from the Indians only "superfluities, as golde, perles, precious stones, and such other," and, he

added almost as an afterthought, Spain also took their freedom and their land. In return, the Spaniards taught the natives how to manure their fields and thus marvelously increased yields; moreover, "Theyr bondage is suche as is much rather to be desired then theyr former libertie." Justice and virtue prevailed: "[T]hanked be God, by the manhodde and pollicie of the Spanyardes, this develysshe generation is so consumed, partely by the slaughter of suche as coulde by no means be brought to civilitie"; the rest were forced into the swelling ranks of Christianity "to the confusion of the Devyll and the Turkysshe Antichryste."[8]

In contrast to Eden's preface, Martyr's text sometimes painted a sympathetic portrait of the Indians. Martyr, like Münster, condemned their cannibalism but underlined its limited practice; he regretted their indolence but praised their generosity; he deplored their ferocity but admired their courage. Still, Martyr could not discard his obsession with Indian nakedness. Again and again, he wrote of "naked inhabytantes," "naked Barbarians," and people of "goodly stature, but naked."[9] On balance, Eden's editions of Münster and Martyr conveyed to the English audience a mixed but predominantly pejorative image of the Indians, as did William Cuningham's *Cosmographical Glasse* (1559), a synthesis of various Continental accounts of the whole world and its peoples. Africans, Asians, Irishmen, and American Indians all fared badly at Cuningham's hands. Indians, he implied, were lawless, belligerent, licentious, and cannibalistic: "Their bread is ro[o]tes, and theyr meate mans fleshe."[10] The Columbian legacy persisted.

Not until the late 1570s did firsthand accounts of Indians by English observers finally reach the public, but they too presented a badly tainted image, modified here and there by dashes of faint praise. In 1577–1578, several reports of Martin Frobisher's expeditions in search of a Northwest Passage lambasted the natives of the far north. Dionyse Settle related (perhaps secondhand) that some of them were "altogether voyde of humanitie, and ignorant what mercy meaneth." (Settle's evidence for the Americans' ignorance of mercy was curious: several natives killed themselves rather than submit to seizure by the English.)[11] But Settle's picture of the natives was no harsher than those of seaman Thomas Ellis and Captain George Best, who accompanied Frobisher. Ellis characterized the natives he encountered as "a barbarous and uncivill people, Infidels and miscreantes."[12] Best variously labeled them "Caniballs" and "brutish and uncivil," and he decried their lives and manners:

> They live in Caves of the Earth, and hunte for their dinners or praye [prey], even as the Beare, or other wilde beastes do. They eate rawe fleshe and fishe, and refuse no meate, howsoever it be stincking. They are desperate in their fighte, sullen of nature, and ravenous in their manner of feeding.[13]

Thus the earliest direct English observations of Indians were, over all, more derogatory than their Continental precursors.

Even the younger Richard Hakluyt, who in 1582 entered the literary scene that he would dominate until the dawn of the new century with voluminous publications on international exploration and colonization, joined the consensus. Hakluyt's elder cousin, also named Richard, had strongly encouraged English colonization of America, but he published little on the subject; his major contribution to the imperialist trend was to excite the younger Hakluyt's interest in collecting and publishing the narratives of English exploration. The first of his collections, *Divers Voyages Touching the Discoverie of America*, contained Continental narratives as well and thus reiterated the traditional stereotypes of American natives. Almost a century of European writings had only reinforced the largely derogatory image that Columbus initiated and his successors perpetuated. Yet only a year after Hakluyt's first publication, several English-language works heralded the gradual emergence of a substantially different message.

The shift in English thinking about the Indians that began in 1583 had several sources. One was the growing conflict between the Catholic and Protestant branches of Christianity and the interwoven rivalry between Spain and England. In the propaganda war Protestant writers seized as ammunition the traditional Spanish story—the glory of their New World conquests and the Indians' barbarity as the justification for Spain's actions—but reversed the scenario's moral positions. Rather than portraying the Indians as evil and the Spanish as valiantly and righteously victorious, as Richard Eden had suggested in 1555, English accounts now accused the Spanish of being greedy and bloodthirsty at the expense of Indians, who were represented as innocent and gentle. The "Black Legend" of extreme Spanish cruelty was born.

Damning the Spanish and obliquely praising the Indians was only the first step in the changing assessment of the American natives, for English writers insisted that the Indians still needed civility and Christianity. But they predicted that the Indians' hatred of the Spanish would lead inexorably to the Indians' love for the English and *their* version of Christianity. (The possibility that America's natives might prefer no European neighbors or beliefs rarely surfaced.) As early as 1584 the younger Hakluyt wrote with undocumented optimism that "the people of America crye oute unto us their nexte neighboures to come and helpe them, and bringe unto them the gladd tidinges of the gospell."[14] His elder cousin agreed: The people in the area coveted by England are "of a mylde and tractable disposition, apte to submytte them selves to good government, and ready to imbrace the christian faythe."[15]

Several English-language publications mark the trend toward a more benign assessment of the Indians. One was the first English translation of the scathing indictment of the Spanish conquest by the Dominican bishop Bartolomé de Las Casas. It was not only a shocking exposé of "Spanish Cruelties" (the running head on every page) but also a strong endorsement of the Indians' humanity and docility. In addition, English publishers translated several French accounts by Protestant authors, such as Jean Ribaut, who shared England's anti-Catholic stance and described the Indians in terms that were generally tolerant and hopeful rather than scornful.

English authors simultaneously reflected the new trend. George Peckham, in his *True Reporte . . . of the Newfound Landes* (1583), gave scant attention to the Indians, but in attempting to encourage and justify settlement among them, he emphasized the Indians' potential for civil behavior and religious conversion and hinted at their eventual amalgamation with the Anglo-American settlements that Peckham and other imperialists advocated. Under English tutelage, he predicted, the Indians "shalbe reduced from unseemly customes, to honest maners, from disordred riotous rowtes and companies, to a wel governed common wealth, & with all shalbe taught mecanicall occupations, artes, and lyberal Sciences."[16] Other English writers of the 1580s who foreshadowed the benign image included Christopher Carleill, an active participant in English expansion overseas; he expected the Indians to "daily by little and little forsake their barbarous and savage living, and growe to . . . order and civilitie with us."[17] The cumulative effect of these writings, despite their palpable paternalism and imperialism, encouraged the English public to think more favorably of the Indians.

Another influence on England's changing perceptions was her belated entrance into the European race for a New World empire. England needed colonists to make her imperial scheme work, for without farmers and laborers, colonies could not survive, and without some prospect of friendly relations with the Indians, few Englishmen would migrate to America. Consequently, it became fashionable to see the Indians as similar to themselves, rather than different. English references to Indians increasingly stressed fundamental correspondences between Indians and Englishmen in appearance and character, an emphasis that benefited from the more frequent visits by Indians to England, where the English could see—as a few of their ancestors had in 1502 and occasionally thereafter—that, except for the superficialities of clothing and body paint, Indians were very much like themselves. In 1616–1617 Pocahontas played the Anglicized Indian's role extremely well: she was now the Lady Rebecca, wife of John Rolfe, dressing in English finery and speaking the language of Shakespeare and Jonson. Other Indians in England created less excitement but carried the same implicit message.

A cornerstone of the new perception was a growing consensus that the Indians were innately white-skinned; they appeared brown or tawny only because they stained their bodies with penetrating juices and were perpetually tanned by the sun. English writers as diverse and knowledgeable as John Smith, William Strachey, and John Rolfe of Virginia; William Wood, Thomas Morton, and Roger Williams of New England; George Alsop of Maryland; and William Penn of Pennsylvania agreed on this point, if on nothing else. Morton, after spending several years in Massachusetts, explained that Indian infants were born as white as English children but that their mothers made a special concoction to "staine their skinne for ever, wherein they dip and washe them to make them tawny."[18] Corroboration came from observers in England, who testified that visiting Indians who adopted English clothing and abjured body stains soon lost much or all of their distinctive color. William Crashaw, a London clergyman and colonial promoter, told of "a Virginian [Indian], that was with us here in *England*, whose skinne (though hee had gone naked all his life, till our men persuaded him to bee clothed) . . . was little more blacke or tawnie, than one of ours would be if he should goe naked in the South of *England*."[19] There was, in sum, no significant difference in pigmentation between Indians and Englishmen; one could wash the Americans white.

English history reinforced the expectation that the Indians would soon be civilized and converted. Had not the English themselves been barbarians until the Romans coerced them into the Christian faith and proper behavior? Early in the 17th century, Crashaw voiced a frequent refrain of English imperialist writings from about 1590 to 1630 when he explained an important parallel between Englishmen and Indians: "[W]e were savage and uncivill, and worshipped the devill, as now they do, then God sent some to make us civill, and others to make us christians."[20] Surely, English spokesmen argued, Indians would respond as the ancient Britons had. Some commentators thought force might be necessary to accomplish that goal (as it had been for the Romans); others expected patience and good example to persuade the Indians to adopt English ways and beliefs. Virtually all spokesmen agreed that the desired outcome was likely if not inevitable.

Portrait of Pocahontas in her English clothing from Captain John Smith, *The Generall Historie of Virginia* (London, 1624).

English attempts to establish and maintain a colony on Roanoke Island in the 1580s left two important contributions to that expectation: John White's superb watercolor paintings of natives in the Roanoke area (cat. nos. 16–19) and Thomas Harriot's detailed account of Indian-English relations, entitled *A briefe and true report*. Both the illustrations and the text reached large audiences during the next several decades. Harriot also wrote "a large discourse" on the Indians that was never published and no longer survives; it may have circulated widely in manuscript and, presumably, furthered the new image.

Harriot's *Briefe and true report* admitted that some Roanoke tribes were hostile to colonization, but he portrayed even them as harmless: their weapons were wooden bows and clubs, bark shields, and armor made of sticks. Indian villages were small and largely unprotected; their government was fragmented; their languages differed from tribe to tribe. Moreover, Harriot recounted, sudden epidemics almost paralyzed Indian resistance, especially in villages recently visited by the colonists, which, he believed, had conspired against the English. In sum, the Indians "are not to be feared"; they were awestruck by the newcomers and powerless to resist them. "[T]here is good hope," Harriot concluded, that "they may be brought through discreet dealing and governement to the imbracing of the trueth, and consequently to honour, obey, feare and love us."[21]

"A cheiff Lorde of Roanoac" from Thomas Harriot, *A briefe and true report* (Frankfurt, 1590).

Two years after the quarto edition of Harriot's book appeared, the Flemish publishers Theodor de Bry and sons issued folio reprints in German, Latin, and English, with 23 engravings based on John White's paintings. Each plate carried an extensive caption, very likely by the younger Hakluyt, who included the English version (but not the illustrations) in his *Principall Navigations* (1589) and again in the third volume of his expanded collection (1600). The frequent reissues of Harriot's book and its inclusion in two such notable series as de Bry's *Americae* and Hakluyt's *Principall Navigations* suggest that it was one of the most widely read secular works of late Elizabethan England. English imperial propaganda had been impressively launched.

The image of the Indians projected by White's paintings was even more benign than the one in Harriot's text. White's Indians are neither threatening nor very "savage." He shows no cannibalism, no torture, no warfare, no crude customs. And although his Indians are largely naked, they are more modestly covered by skins and beads than are the natives in most 16th-century illustrations. White's implicit message is that the natives of southern Virginia are peaceful, orderly, and amenable to "civility." Yet ambiguity once again intrudes. Some English men and women, almost all of them gentry, undoubtedly saw John White's watercolors, but most of the viewers of White's images (many of them, perhaps, illiterate) saw them only in de Bry's engravings and probably absorbed a dual image: on the one hand, the docility of White's natives, and, on the other hand, the contrary depiction of Indians in the numerous other illustrations in the 13 volumes of voyage literature that de Bry and his sons published between 1590 and 1634. There, as before, the viewer encountered cannibalism, cruelty, and stark nakedness.[22]

The first century of English colonization did not, by and large, strengthen the trend of the late 16th and early 17th centuries to see the Indians as friendly, convertible to Christianity, and essentially similar to Europeans. In Virginia, England's first permanent colony, disillusion set in quickly, both among the Indians, who soon saw the disadvantage of having an English settlement in their midst, and among the colonists and their backers at home, who found life in America harder, and profits fewer, than they had expected. The dominant theme became collision rather than conversion.

Indians in most areas of English settlement quickly abandoned their early favorable response to English colonization. Trade with the newcomers had been welcome, but it carried too high a price in lands lost, jurisdiction preempted, and abuses endured. The more the Indians saw of English settlement—with a few ambiguous exceptions—the less tractable they became. Simultaneously, the colonists on the scene and the imperialists back home lost their optimism. The hopeful view of the Indians evaporated slowly at first, then precipitously after the Powhatan uprising of 1622 almost annihilated the Virginia colony; English attitudes reverted with a vengeance to their earlier emphasis on Indian treachery and cruelty. Samuel Purchas, Hakluyt's successor as England's principal imperial propagandist, concluded that Virginia's Indians had "little of Humanitie but shape, [were] ignorant of Civilitie, of Arts, of Religion; more brutish then the beasts they hunt."[23]

Despite some temporary countertrends, the early English optimism of the late 16th and early 17th centuries concerning conversion and Anglicization continued to erode, especially as Indian resistance accelerated. It seemed to English eyes that Indians stubbornly resisted Christianity and deprecated English customs. They fought against the English in brutal wars, thwarted English territorial

expansion, and rejected English hegemony. Along the way, the suspicion grew, especially among Englishmen overseas, that the Indians were after all not innately white but were one of humankind's dark-skinned races, destined to subservience and contempt. Indians captured in war—or, more often, purchased from other Indians—were increasingly thrust into slavery, where they merged with Africans imported for the same sorry purpose. By the last decades of the century, a conflation of Indian and African images was underway that can be seen in European paintings that mix the two peoples' representative facial features, pigmentation, and artifacts. The conflation is also reflected in colonial laws that lump Indians and Africans together as the objects of special discrimination.

As time went on, some Anglo-American observers feared that Indian ways were subverting colonial civility rather than the latter uplifting the natives; atavism among the settlers seemed frightfully evident. Increase Mather, the prominent New England clergyman, lamented in 1679 that "People are ready to run wild into the woods . . . and to be as heathenish as ever, if you doe not prevent it."[24] Two decades later, his son Cotton Mather complained: "We have too far degenerated into *Indian* Vices. . . . We have shamefully Indianized."[25] The Mathers were reflecting the especially pessimistic outlook of the last quarter of the 17th century, when the pendulum was swinging strongly toward the pejorative view and the prevailing colonial perception of the Indian was once again almost wholly negative. But that view was not necessarily current in England, where yet another strand of changing perceptions of American natives was emerging. While many, if not most, Anglo-Americans were becoming more pessimistic about the prospect that Indians would embrace English forms of Christianity and social behavior and increasingly resorted to racist analyses of Indian culture, many English men and women remained excited about their Indian visitors and accorded them something of a hero's status, foreshadowing the image of the noble savage that would characterize mid-18th century European perceptions of American natives.

Dark-skinned Mexican Indians showing the conflation of Indian and
African characteristics, from Arnoldus Montanus, *De Nieuwe en
Onbekende Weereld* (Amsterdam, 1671).

The resurgence of English curiosity about Indians blended with an emerging glorification of them in 1710, when four Iroquois sachems, or chiefs, journeyed to England as a colonial publicity ploy to win Queen Anne's support for an assault on French Canada. During their brief stay in England, the "Canadian kings," as they were inaccurately known, enthralled London. Dignitaries entertained them with puppet shows and cockfights; Simon Verelst, a distinguished artist, painted their portraits, which in turn were copied by innumerable engravers; crowds gathered wherever the Indians went. At a performance of *Macbeth* on April 24, 1710, a mob in the gallery stopped the show until the "Canadian kings" were seated in clear view on the edge of the stage. Shakespeare's comment of a

century earlier about the curiosity value of Indians in England remained apt. American natives were still the New World's greatest wonder, even though their true nature continued to evade Europe's—even European America's—comprehension.

Alden T. Vaughan is Professor of History, Columbia University, New York City

Notes

1. J. M. Cohen, ed. and trans., *The Four Voyages of Christopher Columbus: Being His Own Log-Book, Letters and Dispatches* . . . (London: Penguin Books, 1969), pp. 117, 116, 120, 67.

2. Cohen, ed., *Four Voyages of Columbus*, p. 66.

3. The pioneer account of the hemispheric differences and their post-1492 effects is Alfred W. Crosby, Jr., *The Columbian Exchange: Biological and Cultural Consequences of 1492* (Westport, Conn.: Greenwood Publishing Co., 1972). See also Herman J. Viola and Carolyn Margolis, eds., *Seeds of Change: A Quincentennial Commemorative* (Washington, D.C.: Smithsonian Institution Press, 1991).

4. Samuel Eliot Morison, ed. and trans., *Journals and Other Documents on the Life and Voyages of Christopher Columbus* (New York: Heritage Press, 1963), pp. 180–186.

5. James A. Williamson, ed., *The Cabot Voyages and Bristol Discovery under Henry VII* (Cambridge: Cambridge University Press for the Hakluyt Society, 1962), p. 220; Richard Hakluyt, *Divers Voyages Touching the Discoverie of America* (London: for Thomas Woodcocke by Thomas Dawson, 1582), sigs. A3–A3ᵛ.

6. Edward Arber, ed., *The First Three English Books on America, [?1511–1555 A.D.]* (Birmingham, Eng., 1885), pp. xxvii–xxxvi.

7. *The Letters of Amerigo Vespucci and Other Documents*, trans. Clements R. Markham (London: for the Hakluyt Society, 1894), p. 47.

8. Peter Martyr, *The Decades of the Newe Worlde or West India*, trans. Richard Eden (London: by Edward Sutton, 1555), sigs. [aiiᵛ–aiii].

9. Martyr, *Decades of the Newe Worlde*, sigs. 134ᵛ, 114ᵛ, 52, and passim.

10. William Cuningham, *The Cosmographical Glasse, Conteinyng the Principles of Cosmographie, Geographie, Hydrographie, or Navigation* (London: John Day, 1559), p. 201.

11. Dionyse Settle, *A True Reporte of the Last Voyage into the West and Northwest Regions . . . by Capteine Frobisher* (London: Henry Middleton, 1577), sig. C1.

12. Thomas Ellis, *A True Report of the Third and Last Voyage into Meta Incognita* (London: T. Dawson, 1578), sig. [B6].

13. George Best, *A True Discourse of the Late Voyages of Discoverie, for the Finding of a Passage to Cathaya, by the Northweast* (London: Henry Bynneman, 1578), p. 62.

14. E. G. R. Taylor, ed., *The Original Writings and Correspondence of the Two Richard Hakluyts* (London: for the Hakluyt Society, 1935), vol. 2, p. 216.

15. Taylor, ed., *Writings of the Two Richard Hakluyts*, vol. 2, p. 339.

16. George Peckham, *A True Reporte of the Late Discoveries, and Possession, Taken in the Right of the Crowne of Englande, of the Newfound Landes* . . . (London: by I. C. for John Hinde, 1583), sigs. Fiii–Fiiiᵛ.

17. Christopher Carleill, "A Briefe and Summary Discourse upon the Intended Voyage to the Hithermost Parts of America," in David B. Quinn, ed., *The Voyages and Colonising Enterprises of Sir Humphrey Gilbert* (London: The Hakluyt Society, 1940), vol. 2, p. 357.

18. Thomas Morton, *New English Canaan* (Amsterdam: Jacob Frederick Stam, 1637), p. 32.

19. William Crashaw, *A Sermon Preached in London before the Right Honourable Lord La Warre* . . . (London: for William Welby, 1610), sig. E2.

20. Crashaw, *Sermon Preached in London*, sig. C4ᵛ.

21. Thomas Harriot, *A briefe and true report of the new found land of Virginia* (Frankfurt am Main: Johann Wechel for Theodor de Bry, 1590), pp. 24, 29.

22. In addition to the many de Bry volumes themselves, see esp. Bernadette Bucher, *Icon and Conquest: A Structural Analysis of the Illustrations of deBry's Great Voyages*, trans. Basia Miller Gulati (Chicago: University of Chicago Press, 1981).

23. Samuel Purchas, *Hakluytus Posthumus, or Purchas His Pilgrimes: Contayninge a History of the World in Sea Voyages and Lande Travells* . . . (1625; Glasgow: J. MacLehose and Sons, 1906), vol. 19, p. 231.

24. Increase Mather, *A Discourse Concerning the Danger of Apostacy* (Boston, 1679), p. 75.

25. Cotton Mather, *Magnalia Christi Americana: or the Ecclesiastical History of New-England* . . . (London: for T. Parkhurst, 1702), bk. 6, p. 35.

The first European depiction of Native Americans: Taino Indians of Hispaniola in a woodcut issued with the 1493 Basel edition of Columbus's letter announcing his discoveries. Reproduced with the permission of the Rare Books and Manuscripts Division, The New York Public Library, Astor, Lenox and Tilden Foundations.

The Sources for European Imagery of Native Americans

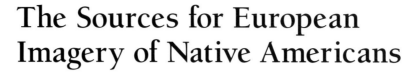

William C. Sturtevant

4, 1493, Columbus arrived in Lisbon ʳˢt report of his discoveries, in the r. By mid-April this report, which ˢt European description of Amer- ᵘblished, and within a year ten ᵢₛ had appeared, in Spanish, Latin, ₐn, and German. Although the first versions were not illustrated, woodcuts were soon added, first in a Latin edition of Columbus's letter issued in Basel in 1493 and 1494, and then in versified Italian editions published in 1493 and 1495.[1]

It is readily apparent, now, that the first pictures published with the letter were based on American reality only insofar as Columbus's brief verbal descriptions allowed; this limitation was often the case with later depictions of Americans as well. Columbus gave very little specific information about the appearance of the people he encountered. He did write that "the people of the island [of Hispaniola] and all the others that I have found and heard about all go naked, men and women, just as their mothers bore them, although some women cover themselves in one spot with a plant leaf or a net of cotton which they make for that purpose." Thus, when the first European illustrators of his letter showed a small crowd of Indians, they were depicted as unclothed except for the brief belts or girdles of leaves worn by some of the women. These belts are suspiciously similar to those worn by some of the Wild People of medieval and post-medieval European legend; they do not resemble the cache-sexes of later Indians of tropical South America.

Only two other Indian artifacts are depicted in these woodcuts: a few simple sheds (which are unlike what little is known of the houses of the Taino Indians of the Greater Antilles) and the long poles carried by a few of the men. In one woodcut these poles are clearly shown to be made of cane or bamboo, whereas in another version they are plain poles with short crosspieces near the tips. In his letter, Columbus said that the Taino "have no weapons except those of canes [cut] when in seed, on the end of which they put a little sharp stick."[2] The crosspieces shown on the spears are surely wrong: later evidence on Indian weapons from culturally similar regions indicates that Columbus must have intended to describe a sharp wooden spearhead, not an axelike crosspiece. In addition, several of the men in the woodcuts are shown with full beards, which the engravers could not have known were impossible for American Indian men. Similarly, several Indians seem to have wavy hair, also highly improbable for Native Americans. In the 1495 woodcuts the Indians have long hair, although when Columbus specified that the Caribs had long hair he evidently implied a contrast with the Taino (shown here), who may have worn their hair shorter.[3]

Although Columbus returned to Europe with more than ten Taino Indians and a number of Indian artifacts—seen by vast crowds in Portugal and Spain—it is clear that the first European illustrations did not draw on this visual evidence. Rather, the artists simply modified traditional European imagery, attempting to follow the verbal descriptions in the texts they were

Taino Indians in a woodcut from the version of Columbus's letter published in Florence in 1495. Reproduced with the permission of the Biblioteca Trivulziana, Milan.

illustrating. Some, of course, did not do even that but merely borrowed, without making any changes, illustrations that had been prepared for other purposes. The scarcity of European visual depictions based even indirectly on Taino reality is tragic, for shockingly soon that reality no longer existed: by 1550 the aboriginal cultures and most of the native peoples of the Greater Antilles had been totally destroyed.

Among the very few accurate depictions of Taino culture are ten drawings, mostly of artifacts, made by the chronicler Gonzalo Fernández de Oviedo after spending about twenty years in Santo Domingo, beginning in 1514. Woodcuts after nine of these drawings were published in 1526 and 1539 in Oviedo's books on natural history, along with a great many others based on his drawings of New World plants and animals. His Taino pictures had very little influence, however, probably because Oviedo was not a skilled artist (as he himself admitted) and because only a couple of his woodcuts depict activities, and these were not the sort to arouse

much European interest: a man paddling a canoe and a crude scene of gold washing. Most of Oviedo's original drawings survive but even now have not been published.[4]

Reports of the Tupinamba Indians of coastal Brazil, by contrast, very quickly aroused European interest. These Indians were first seen by Europeans in 1500 when Pedro Álvares Cabral accidentally struck Brazil on his way around Africa to India. He sent a ship back to Portugal with a letter announcing the discovery to the king, in which Pêro Vaz de Caminha described the natives:

> They were dark and entirely naked, without anything to cover their shame. They carried in their hands bows with their arrows. All came boldly towards the boat, and Nicolau Coelho made a sign to them that they should lay down their bows, and they laid them down. He could not have any speech with them there, nor understanding which might be profitable, because of the breaking of the sea on the shore. He gave them only a red cap and a cap of linen, which he was wearing on his head, and a black hat. And one of them gave him a hat of long bird feathers with a little tuft of red and grey feathers like those of a parrot. And another gave him a large string of very small white beads which look like seed pearls. . . . They seem to me a people of such innocence that, if one could understand them and they us, they would soon be Christians. . . . For it is certain this people is good and of pure simplicity, and there can easily be stamped upon them whatever belief we wish to give them; and furthermore, Our Lord gave them fine bodies and good faces as to good men; and He who brought us here, I believe, did not do so without purpose.[5]

From this passage it is easy for us to see the beginnings of many misunderstandings about the Indians on the part of Europeans, including those regarding the idea of Indians as Noble Savages. Cabral sent back Tupinamba featherwork and other objects, and very soon illustrations appeared with realistic Tupinamba ornaments and weapons—the first European depictions of Native American artifacts done from life. It was, however, a long time before credible portraits of the Indians themselves were done. In the 16th century even the most skillful artists drew Americans with the proportions of classical sculpture.

The earliest known illustrations of Tupinamba artifacts appear in a Portuguese altarpiece painted in oils and in a colored woodblock print published in Augsburg.[6] Neither is securely dated, but both seem to have been done in 1505. The print accompanies a short text in German based on a French version of a letter written in Italian by Amerigo Vespucci. Illustrating the text beneath it, the scene shows a group of eleven Indians: three men with weapons, a woman with three children, another woman holding a cornstalk, and a group engaged in a cannibalistic feast. The cornstalk looks more like millet than corn, the men have non-Indian beards, and the human body parts being eaten are not butchered and prepared as they must certainly have been in reality. There is ample evidence for customary cannibalism among the Tupinamba, however, and this was surely an important element in their notoriety in Europe.

The feather ornaments worn by the Indians, however, are rather accurately depicted.[7] These include vertical crowns, short capes or large collars, arm and ankle bands, and skirts of long feathers. The artist who did the woodcut must have had before him either sketches or, more likely, actual examples of the objects, which were probably sent directly to Augsburg from Portugal rather than accompanying the text. A woman in the print wears a feather bustle in the form of a rosette, which is known to be an ornament worn by Tupinamba men, not women. There are many parallels among modern Brazilian Indians for the feather crowns, capes, and bands on arms and legs, documented by museum specimens, photographs, and anthropological observation. They are often shown in early drawings and prints as well. Many Tupinamba examples entered European cabinets of curiosities—the most important surviving pieces are in the Danish national museum—before the end of the 17th century; by that time the Tupinamba had ceased to exist as distinct cultural groups.

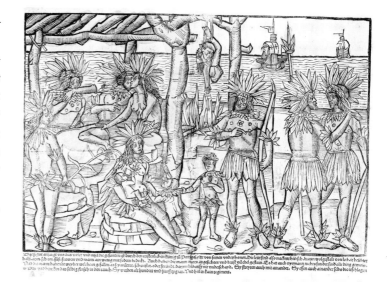

Tupinamba Indians of coastal Brazil in a woodcut printed in Augsburg, probably in 1505. Reproduced with the permission of the Bayerische Staatsbibliothek, Munich.

The feather skirts in the Augsburg print are not mentioned in the quite full written evidence on Tupinamba customs; none of them survive in museum collections; and very few appear in early depictions that otherwise seem reliable. Awkward as they must have been to wear, they are nevertheless believable for several reasons. A few examples are known among modern Brazilian Indians; they can be considered to be rare variants of the belts made of shorter feathers that are among the Tupinamba objects in Copenhagen and that are used by some modern Brazilian Indians; they appear in a Tupinamba dance scene shown on a 16th-century map that otherwise seems to be based on firsthand observation;[8] and one or more were apparently part of the collections available a few years after 1505 to artists working for the Holy Roman Emperor Maximilian I.[9]

The oil painting of 1505 shows one of the three Magi as an Indian rather than an African king. He appears in a somewhat brief costume of sumptuous European (or perhaps oriental) cloth with several typically Brazilian attributes that can only have been based on Tupinamba artifacts brought to Portugal: a radial feather crown in front of a downy feather cap; a very long, heavily

An American as one of the Three Kings, in an altar painting of about 1505 from the cathedral of Viseu, Portugal. Reproduced with the permission of Museo de Grão Vasco, Viseu.

fletched arrow; and a belt and necklace both of short feathers. His bead necklaces may also be from the Tupinamba. Although the king does not have especially Indian features, the artist may have seen Indians because the skin color seems to be American rather than African or European. It has been suggested that an American could appear as one of the Magi after the accounts of Cabral's friendly relations with the Brazilians were known, but hardly after Vespucci and others reported their cannibalism.[10] Even though the artist probably knew of Tupinamba nakedness, its depiction was inappropriate in this context.

Soon after these first pictures, other appropriately Tupinamba characteristics appeared in European imagery. Indian nakedness could, of course, be depicted solely on the basis of verbal descriptions. Two types of Brazilian clubs were shown so accurately, however, that the artists must have seen actual examples. One of these clubs, with a long handle and a paddle-shaped

blade, was used by the Tupinamba in battle and for the ritual sacrifice of war captives before they were eaten (see p. 115, Vaughan, "Salvages and Men of Ind," below). Many of these clubs were collected as souvenirs and trophies, and at least ten have been preserved in old European collections, including the cabinet of the Bibliothèque Sainte-Geneviève in Paris (see cat. nos. 47 and 52). Complicating the issue, however, is the fact that not one of these clubs—and none of the surviving Tupinamba feather ornaments—has a recorded history tracing it to a Tupinamba origin, or even indicating that it probably came from Brazil. Attribution to the Tupinamba depends on 16th-century depictions of Indian clubs with this very distinctive shape, some of them accompanied by written descriptions of their use. The other club type that often appears in illustrations is the so-called anchor axe, which is known from examples collected later in the interior of Brazil but which may well have also been a Tupinamba type, since it appears in pictures made while European contacts were largely restricted to the coast (see cat. no. 51).[11]

The Tupinamba crown of vertical feathers and the skirt made of feathers were soon incorporated into the repertoire of European art and popular imagery. They came to indicate Indian identity in most parts of the Americas until well into the 19th century, despite their actual limitation to coastal Brazil and the probability that among the Tupinamba the feather skirt was a man's ornament worn only on infrequent and special occasions. In European art these feather ornaments were developed into new and more elaborate forms. The skirt, originally a row of long, straight feathers, was often shown as a kind of fabric of overlapping rows of small feathers. The upright feathers of the crown sometimes became fluffy ostrich or egret plumes, and the headgear was often changed into a more complex structure.

The feather crown and feather skirt and some other Brazilian elements were selected to typify America as one of the four continents in an iconographic scheme that became popular after about 1570. Each continent was represented by an alle-

The only surviving Tupinamba feather crown, made of red and blue macaw tail-feathers about 2 feet long. It was received by the Danish Royal Cabinet of Curiosities before 1690. Reproduced with the permission of The National Museum of Denmark, Department of Ethnography.

gorical figure, nearly always female, consistent with the feminine gender of the Latin names for the continents. For this reason, "Amerigo" (Vespucci) was changed to "America." Europe and Asia usually appear as fully clothed figures, despite their customary classical drapery and poses. Africa is less covered, and America still less, and often appears completely nude. These stereotypes partly reflect ethnographic reality, for in both the American and the African tropics people normally exposed most of their bodies. In addition, each figure is usually accompanied by an identifying animal. For Europe this is most often a bull, alluding to the Greek myth in which Europa was carried off by Zeus who had taken the form of a bull. Nonetheless, sometimes the European animal is a horse. Asia usually appears with a camel or a lion, but sometimes with an elephant, rhinoceros, or parrot, while Africa is accompanied by an elephant, lion, or crocodile. For America the identifying animal is an armadillo or a crocodile,

but sometimes a parrot. Weapons may also be shown, often merely a bow and arrow (occasionally with a quiver) for each continent, but for America frequently one of the two distinctive Tupinamba clubs. Each figure may have other identifying attributes. Europe may have a crown and scepter, while Asia wears a turban and Africa a headcloth. Africa is sometimes shaded by a parasol, while Europe may have a cornucopia and Asia a censer. America is often accompanied by a severed head or another human body part, to symbolize the cannibalism found among the Tupinamba and then extended to be a general American characteristic. But the most constant attribute of America is the feather decoration. America is almost always shown wearing a feather crown, a feather skirt, or both, and these are ultimately of Tupinamba origin (see cat. nos. 3, 55, and 81–84).[12]

The allegorical figure of America was developed in concert with those of the other three continents, but it went on to have an independent career as a symbol for America as a whole, or for American Indians in any part of the Americas. The figure even appears in the 18th century as an allegorical allusion to the separation of the North American colonists from their English rulers.[13]

The Tupinamba vertical feather crown is still with us, in a sense, for the modern Indian "war bonnet" of eagle feathers is probably a derivative. The Tupinamba crown spread as the European and Euro-American stereotype of Indian appearance until it influenced the choice of a somewhat similar Plains Indian feather headgear as a replacement. The new stereotype of Indian identity was adopted by many North American Indians themselves in the late 19th and early 20th centuries. It is now perhaps the only visual stereotype of ethnicity that remains generally acceptable.[14]

That clothing and personal adornment indicate social and cultural characteristics is an ancient European idea. It seems to have seriously misled observers of the Tupinamba. The fact that they wore no clothes meant to the Europeans that the Tupinamba existed in a state of nature. Since they had no clothes, it was supposed that they also had no rulers, laws, and religion. By the time European observers became better informed, the idea of the Noble Savage, based largely on the first reports of the Tupinamba, had taken on an independent existence. In fact, according to modern anthropological scales of socio-political complexity, the Tupinamba fall somewhere at the upper level of tribal organization, just below the chiefdom level.[15]

On the other hand, the Eskimos (often now called Inuit), who were first encountered by Europeans in Labrador and Baffinland in the 16th century and in Greenland soon thereafter, were not organized as tribes at all but lived in true band-level societies, without rulers or laws in the European sense. They were more nearly Noble Savages than any Indians known to Europeans for the next couple of hundred years. Yet, because they lived in the Arctic, they were fully clothed and were thus depicted by European artists. Eskimos very rarely fill allegorical roles, and their appearance has not been affected by European ideas about how Native Americans should look. Their environment, considered harsh by Europeans, protected them until modern times from the destruction visited on all other Native American cultures by European and Euro-American explorers, conquerors, and settlers. Because most of the material aspects of Inuit cultures persisted until very recent times, the details of their arts and manufactures are much better known to anthropologists than are those of the other inhabitants of the eastern seaboards of the American continents. Many typical Inuit objects are in museum collections, and anthropologists have assembled a large, detailed descriptive literature, including photographs. It is therefore much easier to evaluate the accuracy of early European depictions of Inuit dress, housing, weapons, and other implements. Images documenting Inuit cultures were generally more precise than were pictures of the ways of other Native Americans, perhaps because European observers were especially interested in recording Inuit techniques for survival in the Arctic, which European explorers consistently adopted.[16]

The differentiation of clothing according to region, social status, occupation, and occasion had been especially important to Europeans since about

Athabalippa Rex vltimus America.

The Inca emperor Atahualpa as depicted in de Bruyn's costume book published in 1581 (cat. no. 40).

the middle of the 14th century, because dress and adornment were believed to indicate social characteristics of people. By the middle of the 16th century "national" costumes in Europe had stabilized, and serious travelers and explorers recorded the details they observed. There soon arose a need to inventory and classify these details of dress. One of the first systematizers was Christoph Weiditz, an artist from Augsburg who traveled with the court of Charles V in Spain and the Netherlands between 1529 and 1532, recording in watercolors the costumes of various regions and occupations, of African slaves and the Moors of Granada, and of a group of Aztecs brought to the court by Cortés. Although they were not published until the 20th century, Weiditz's illustrations must have circulated widely, for copies can be recognized in several of the costume books published in Germany, France, Italy, and the Netherlands during the succeeding century.[17] Among those who used Weiditz's work were Hans Weigel and Jost Amman, whose engravings in turn were among the sources for the costume books published by Abraham de Bruyn in 1577 and thereafter (see cat. no. 40).

Costume books were evidently used as printed compendia of social characteristics around the world. The engravings in them were based, usually without acknowledgment, on published illustrations in other costume books, in accounts of voyages, and on other pictorial sources. Occasionally a nonprinted source, such as a drawing in a manuscript, seems to have disappeared, making evaluation of the accuracy of the image difficult, since the compilers of the volumes often greatly modified the details of dress shown in their sources and frequently used captions to assign figures to regions distant from their original ones. Yet sometimes a detail seems to be approximately correct while no earlier source is known. An example is de Bruyn's depiction of the Inca emperor Atahualpa, who holds a staff that must represent the royal symbol called *suntur paucar* by the Incas. This is most curious, since the earliest known depictions of this symbol appear in drawings by the native Andean artist Felipe Guaman Poma de Ayala that were finished only in 1615.[18] De Bruyn must have followed a source that has since disappeared. His Atahualpa also wears feather ornaments ultimately based on illustrations of the Tupinamba. Earlier models for these are obvious, except that the ends of the feathers of a typical Tupinamba cape or headdress that project behind his knees seem not to be otherwise documented before the 17th century.

Costume books were supplemented and then replaced by illustrated collections of accounts of voyages. By far the most influential of these was the series published by the de Bry family between 1590 and 1634. They covered American voyages in 13 parts, or volumes, with 304 different engravings of American scenes, animals, and plants, the activities of Native Americans, and incidents in European exploration and conquests. In most cases the engravers reworked engravings and woodcuts found in earlier works, usually with greatly improved artistic techniques and with considerable elaboration so as to depict a variety of typical activities and scenes.

The illustrations in the earlier volumes of the de Bry series are far more accurate than nearly all those published in their later volumes. Those in the first volume, issued in 1590, are the best of all. They are based on drawings prepared by John White in 1585 during the failed English attempt to establish a colony at Roanoke, North Carolina (called Virginia at that date, see cat. nos. 16–20). Fortunately, many original watercolors by White survive, so that one can gauge the distorting effects of copying by the engravers, which are occasionally significant. The poses of the Indians, their facial features and body proportions, and the composition of multi-figure scenes are certainly not very realistic. But most of the objects, including clothing and personal ornaments, have close parallels in later, better-known Indian societies of the same general region.[19]

The second volume in the de Bry series is devoted to the French expeditions to northern Florida in 1562 and 1564–1565. The engravings are based on original drawings or watercolors by Jacques le Moyne de Morgues. None of the originals survives, and the published versions must have been elaborated from far fewer examples than was the case with the White drawings. In fact, le Moyne may have provided only a few isolated figures in the style of the costume books, from which the engravers composed illustrations of Indian activities. Directly relevant comparative data are much scarcer than for the White drawings, but the de Bry–le Moyne evidence on the culture of the Timucua Indians of Florida is surely less reliable than the de Bry–White materials on the "Virginia" Indians. The Florida pictures include several elements that appear in later de Bry engravings of the Tupinamba, which must have been carried over from sources that had already been collected for other volumes, because there is no other evidence for the existence of such cultural features in southeastern North America.[20]

When the de Brys turned to printing accounts of explorations in Brazil, they had several published sources to draw on for fairly accurate illustrations of the Tupinamba. These included the remarkable captivity narrative of Hans Staden, published in

1557 with 42 rather crude woodcuts that neverthe-less contain much useful and accurate information. Among other good sources were engravings in the books of André Thevet, issued in 1557–1584, and Jean de Léry, published in 1578. These were based on the authors' own experiences in Brazil with Villegagnon in 1555–1557. That Staden, Thevet, and Léry either were draftsmen themselves or else closely supervised their illustrators is indicated by the comparisons that can be made with surviving Tupinamba artifacts, and with much later evidence on Indian cultures of the Brazilian interior. The de Bry artists used their pictorial sources very cre-atively, elaborating and "improving" many details and recombining figures and elements into new, lively scenes.

As their series moved to regions for which there were fewer pictorial resources, the de Brys simply carried over motifs from their earlier volumes that described quite different cultures. The competence of the engravers remained at a high level, and all the volumes repeatedly served as sources for many later illustrators.[21]

The work of the de Brys was important for establishing a customary manner for representing exotic peoples and their products, and the varying reliability of the images is typical of the time. Although accuracy was certainly a goal of artists in the 16th and 17th centuries, it was very often subordinated to stylistic and compositional consid-erations and was influenced by efforts to address the expectations of the audience. Even for pictures prepared after the development of scientific illustrat-ing, during the late 18th century, in which accu-rate representation is primary, one should not overlook other influences that affect the prepara-tion and presentation of images. After all, not even photography is a faithful reflection of exter-nal reality.

Assessing the accuracy of European represen-tations of Native Americans requires considera-tion of the prevailing stylistic traditions in which the artists worked, as well as the opportunities they had for firsthand observation, in America and in Europe. Available models might have included earlier representations by European art-ists, and Indians and Indian objects viewed in Europe. Sometimes we can assess the accuracy of these early representations by comparing them with actual surviving objects from an appropriate time and place. It is also often useful to compare these early illustrations with evidence on other similar cultures, both contemporary and later. A great deal of helpful material has been compiled through anthropological field and museum research over the past century. Thus it is possi-ble to evaluate the accuracy of European depic-tions of Native American cultural details of the past, despite the tremendous changes and losses these cultures have undergone.

William C. Sturtevant is Curator of North American Ethnology, National Museum of Natural History, Smithsonian Institution, Washington, D.C.

Notes

1. Ricardo E. Alegría, *Las Primeras representaciones gráficas del indio americano, 1493–1523* (San Juan: Instituto de Cultura Puertorriqueña, 1978); Susi Colin, *Das Bild des Indianers im 16. Jahrhundert*, Wissenschaftliche Schriften, Reihe 12, Beiträge zur Kunstgeschichte, vol. 102 (Idstein: Schulz-Kirchner, 1988).

2. *The Four Voyages of Columbus . . . in the Original Spanish, with English Translations*, ed. and trans. Cecil Jane (London, 1930–1933; reprint, New York: Dover Publications, Inc., 1988), pp. 6–9.

3. *The Four Voyages*, pp. 16–17.

4. William C. Sturtevant, "First Visual Images of Native America," in *First Images of America*, ed. Fredi Chiappelli (Berkeley: University of California Press, 1976), pp. 424–425, 447–448.

5. Max Justo Guedes and Gerald Lombardi, eds., *Portugal-Brazil: The Age of Atlantic Discoveries* ([New York]: Bertrand Editora, Franco Maria Ricci, Bra-zilian Cultural Foundation, 1990), p. 162.

6. Fine reproductions appear as items 93 and 129 in *Portugal-Brazil*; the works are discussed by Colin, *Das Bild des Indianers*, pp. 16–17, 186–187, and 331–332, by Sturtevant, "First Visual Images," p. 420, and by Hugh Honour, *The New Golden Land: European Images of America from the Discoveries to the Present Time* (New York: Pantheon Books, 1975), pp. 12 and 53, among others.

7. The standard source on Brazilian Indian feather-work is Berta G. Ribeiro, "Bases para uma classificação dos adornos plumários dos índios do Brasil," in *Suma etnológica brasileira*, ed. Darcy Ribeiro, vol. 3, *Arte Índia* (Petrópolis: FINEP, 1986), pp. 189–226, 55 figs., 8 pls. For all aspects of Tupinamba material culture, the classic monograph by Alfred Métraux, *La Civilisation matérielle des tribus Tupi-Guarani* (Paris: Geuthner, 1928), has not been superseded.

8. See William C. Sturtevant, "The Ethnographical Illustrations," in *The Maps and Text of the Boke of Idrography Presented by Jean Rotz to Henry VIII, now in the British Library*, ed. Helen Wallis (Oxford: Roxburghe Club, 1981), pp. 70–71, referring to drawing by Rotz on map reproduced as pl. 28r.

9. Sturtevant, "First Visual Images," pp. 421–423; Colin, *Das Bild des Indianers*, pp. 332–337.

10. Colin, *Das Bild des Indianers*, p. 331.

11. For surviving Tupinamba clubs, see Christian Feest, "Mexico and South America in the European *Wunderkammer*," in *The Origins of Museums: The Cabinet of Curiosities in Sixteenth- and Seventeenth-Century Europe*, ed. Oliver Impey and Arthur Macgregor (Oxford: Clarendon Press, 1985), pp. 237–244.

12. See Honour, "A Land of Allegory," chap. 4, in *New Golden Land*. The distribution of attributes among the continents is analyzed by Jacques Forge, "L'Image de l'Europe dans la représentation allégorique des quatre continents au 16ème–17ème et 18ème siècles" (Mémoire de maîtrise, Université de Vincennes à Saint-Denis—Paris VIII, 1983).

13. E. McClung Fleming, "The American Image as Indian Princess, 1765–1783," *Winterthur Portfolio* 2 (1965): 65–81.

14. William C. Sturtevant, "La Tupinambisation des Indiens d'Amérique du Nord," in *Les Figures de l'Indien*, ed. Gilles Thérien, Les Cahiers du Département d'études littéraires, no. 9 (Montreal: Université du Québec à Montréal, 1988), pp. 293–303; William C. Sturtevant, "What Does the Plains Indian War Bonnet Communicate?" in *Art as a Means of Communication in Pre-Literate Societies*, ed. Dan Eban (Jerusalem: Israel Museum, 1990), pp. 355–374.

15. William C. Sturtevant, "Tupinamba Chiefdoms?" (Paper presented at symposium, Chiefdoms and Chieftancy: An Integration of Archaeological, Ethnohistorical, and Ethnographic Paradigms, 47th International Congress of Americanists, New Orleans, July 8, 1991).

16. For an example of the use of anthropological evidence in the critical evaluation of early depictions of Eskimos, see William C. Sturtevant and David Beers Quinn, "This New Prey: Eskimos in Europe in 1567, 1576, and 1577," in *Indians and Europe: An Interdisciplinary Collection of Essays*, ed. Christian F. Feest (Aachen: Edition Herodot, Radar Verlag, 1987), pp. 61–140.

17. Daniel Defert, "Un Genre ethnographique profane au XVIe: Les Livres d'habits (Essai d'ethno-iconographie)," in *Histoires de l'anthropologie: XVI–XIX siècles*, ed. Britta Rupp-Eisenreich (Paris: Klincksieck, 1984), pp. 25–41.

18. For the *suntur paucar*, see R. T. Zuidema, "The Royal Whip in Cuzco Art, Social Structure and Cosmology," in *The Language of Things*, ed. Pieter ter Keurs and Dirk Smidt, Mededelingen van het Rijksmuseum voor Volkenkunde, no. 25 (Leiden: Rijksmuseum voor Volkenkunde, 1990), pp. 159–172, esp. pp. 162–164. The identification and the lack of any known model that de Bruyn could have copied were confirmed by Zuidema, letter of 25 May 1992. Guaman Poma's heavily illustrated *Nueva Corónica y buen gobierno* was first published as vol. 23 of the Travaux et Mémoires de l'Institut d'Ethnologie (Paris, 1936; reprint, 1968); there is a critical edition prepared by John V. Murra and Rolena Adorno (Mexico City: Siglo Veintiuno, 1980).

19. Paul Hulton, *America 1585: The Complete Drawings of John White* (Chapel Hill: University of North Carolina Press and British Museum Publications, 1984). More detailed analyses are in Paul Hulton and David Beers Quinn, *The American Drawings of John White, 1577–1590, with Drawings of European and Oriental Subjects* (London: Trustees of the British Museum; Chapel Hill: University of North Carolina Press, 1964).

20. Paul Hulton, ed., *The Work of Jacques Le Moyne de Morgues, a Huguenot Artist in France, Florida and England* (London: British Museum Publications, 1977), and Christian F. Feest, "Jacques Le Moyne Minus Four," *European Review of Native American Studies*, [Budapest], 2, no. 1 (1988): 33–38.

21. The whole series of pictorial works published by the de Brys has not been thoroughly studied. An important, indicative work is by Bernadette Bucher, *Icon and Conquest: A Structural Analysis of the Illustrations of de Bry's Great Voyages* (Chicago and London: University of Chicago Press, 1981); see esp. chap. 1, "Its Authors and Its Public," and chap. 2, "The Makeup of the Mythic Material: Collage and Bricolage." Colin, *Das Bild des Indianers*, contains many identifications of the sources used for de Bry illustrations published before 1600.

New World of Wonders

On March 4, 1493, Christopher Columbus dropped anchor in the port of Lisbon, Portugal. He had just returned from his first voyage to "the Indies," bringing with him seven "Indians" and exciting tales of exotic lands. Two days later he recorded in his journal: "When it was known today that [I] came from the Indies, so many people came from the city of Lisbon to see [me] and to see the Indians, that it was a thing of wonder. They all marveled."

It was the beginning of an age in which Europeans would celebrate wonder and would collect, display, and marvel at the people, works of art, plant and animal specimens, and clothing and implements of other parts of the world. In the 16th and 17th centuries, new discoveries fueled a growing curiosity and an unprecedented interest in collecting information about the customs, dress, and beliefs of other cultures. This interest was motivated at first primarily by a desire to be entertained and was characterized by an emphasis on what was most unusual, but it also led to the beginnings of modern anthropology and the study of the diversity of human cultures.

The novel, the strange, and the exotic were collected, displayed, depicted by artists, and even imitated on the stage. These things draw our attention and cause wonder in us as viewers, and to wonder about something is the first step toward study and learning. The books, engravings, drawings, and artifacts described in the following pages introduce some of the ways in which Europeans first encountered the New World and its peoples. They document and illustrate what it was like, 500 years ago, to wonder at, learn about, visualize, and depict a new world.

1   Claudius Ptolemy (2d cent.)

Geographie opus novissima traductione e Grecorum archetypis castigatissime pressum . . .

Strasbourg, Joannis Schott, 1513

Shelf mark: G 87 P8 L3 1513 Cage

When Columbus made his first landfall on October 12, 1492, he thought he had reached the Indian Ocean, and he referred to the islands he explored as "these Indies." When he actually set foot on the American mainland in 1498, he realized that it was a large continent previously unknown to Europe, a terra incognita. As reports of the newly discovered lands spread, Europeans had to revise their ideas about the size and shape of the world in which they lived.

The most influential work on geography of the ancient and medieval worlds was the *Geographia* of Claudius Ptolemy. The earliest printed version of Ptolemy appeared in 1475. The first important modern edition, prepared by Martin Waldseemüller (1470–1521?), appeared in 1513. It contained new maps, some of them showing the recent discoveries such as the islands of "Isabella" and "Spagnolla" (Española), as well as the vast continent labeled "Terra Incognita." An inscription on this map attributes their discovery to Columbus.

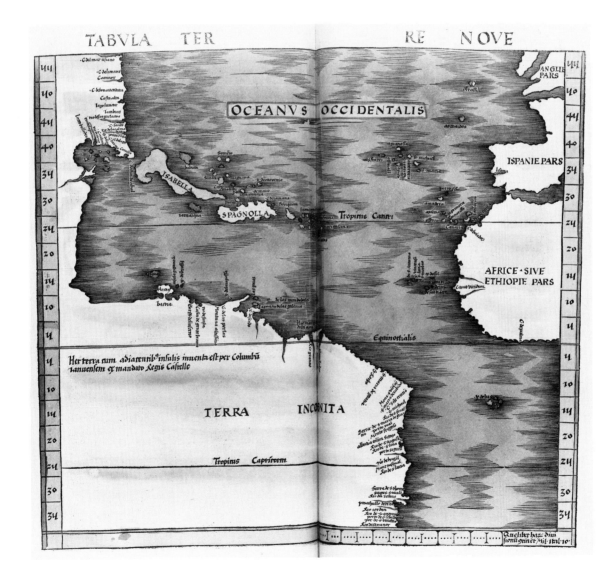

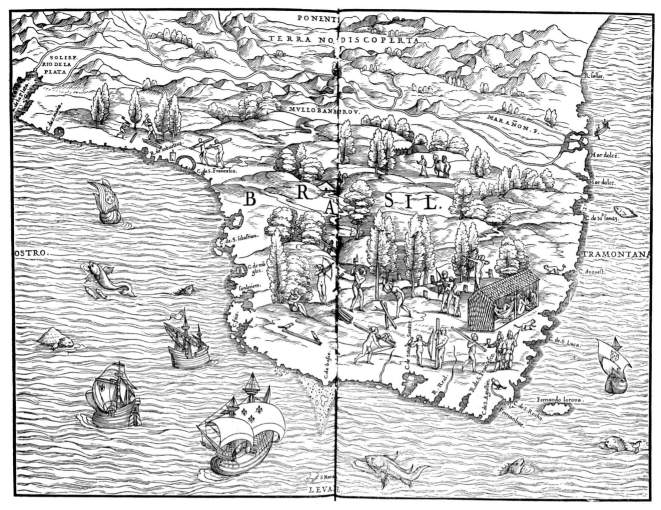

2   Giovanni Battista Ramusio (1485–1557)   N→
Delle Navigationi et Viaggi
Venice, Nella Stamperia de Giunti,
1554–1559
Shelf mark: G 159 R2 1554 Cage

Many of the earliest accounts of the New World described it as a golden land, a paradise with lush vegetation, exotic animals, and naked people who lived in a state of innocence without laws and judges. Most Europeans found it difficult to reconcile these accounts with human history as they knew it from the Bible and the classical writers who had been rediscovered during the Renaissance. Although Europeans had long accepted the existence of Asia and Africa, none of their sources even mentioned this new world, and the land and the people there did not fit into the biblical story of creation and the dispersion of humankind following the flood.

In the middle of the 16th century, Giovanni Battista Ramusio published his large collection of voyages, *Navigationi et Viaggi*, in which he described the most recent travels and discoveries in all parts of the world. His map of eastern Brazil incorporates a crude but fairly accurate illustration of the natives' way of life—their open-sided buildings, the hammocks in which they slept, their weapons and tools, and a lush landscape with birds and animals. It also shows why the natives were interesting to the French; they cut logs of brazilwood and traded them to the French who took them home as a source of red dye for their wool trade.

1.

AMERICA.

Americen Americus retexit, & *Semel vocauit inde semper excitam*.

Ioan: Stradanus inuent.
Theodor Galle sculp. Phls Galle excud.

3   Jan van der Straet (1523–1605)
     Nova reperta

>   Plate 1: *America*
>   Engraved by Théodore and Philippe Galle
>   [Antwerp, c. 1600]
>   Shelf mark: Art vol. f81, plate 1

At the end of the 16th century, the Flemish artist Jan van der Straet produced a series of engravings entitled *Nova reperta* (New discoveries). The first plate in the series, *America*, sums up many of Europe's first images of, and ideas about, the New World. America, a woman newly awakened and vulnerable, dressed only in a feather skirt and cap, is seated on a hammock. Beside her a wooden club, like those used by the Tupinamba Indians of Brazil, rests against a tree. In the surrounding landscape are unusual animals, including an anteater, a

tapir, and a sloth, and in the distance is a group of cannibals. Conflicting images of both innocence and savagery are depicted. Standing before America and dominating the scene is a fully clothed European man, the explorer Amerigo Vespucci.

Van der Straet's *America* illustrates what many Europeans believed—that America was a glorious virgin land waiting to be exploited. In *The Discoverie of the . . . Empire of Guiana* (1596), Sir Walter Raleigh described the land in this way:

>   To conclude, Guiana is a Countrey that hath yet her maydenhead, never sackt, turned, nor wrought, the face of the earth hath not beene torne, nor the vertue and salt of the soyle spent by manurance, the graves have not beene opened for golde, the mines not broken with sledges, nor their Images pulled down out of their temples.

"These Men Were Clothed in Beastes Skinnes"

John Stow, *The Chronicles of England*, 1580

The Indians transported to Lisbon and then to Spain by Columbus were only the first of many taken back to Europe. Over 200 accompanied Amerigo Vespucci on his return from his first voyage in 1499. The Indians, proof that navigators had indeed reached their destinations, were put on display so that the curious could observe them and their clothing, implements, and behavior. Artists drew or painted them, and engravers and printers disseminated these images.

In 1502 Sebastian Cabot presented to King Henry VII of England three men from the northern part of America, probably Newfoundland. They were described by John Stow (1525?–1605) in his *Chronicles of England* (1580):

> Thys yeare were brought unto the Kyng three men taken in the new found Ilands, by Sebastian Gaboto, . . . these men were clothed in beastes skinnes, and eate raw flesh, but spake such a language, as no man could understand them, of the which three men, two of them were seene in the Kings Court at Westminster two yeares after, clothed like Englishmen, and could not bee discerned from Englishmen.

Stow's description, drawn from earlier accounts, emphasized clothing and customs. Although newly discovered cultures were not yet being studied in any systematic way, elements of them were having an impact on the European imagination.

Thomas Wood (16th cent.)
     Manuscript letter to Richard Bagot
          October 10, 1576
          Shelf mark: L.a. 987

On October 9, 1576, Martin Frobisher arrived in London with an Eskimo from Baffin Island. A manuscript journal (now in the British Library) by Michael Lok, one of the backers of Frobisher's voyage, described their reception and "their strannge man & his bote, which was such a wonder unto the whole city." The day after Frobisher's arrival, Thomas Wood wrote a letter to Richard Bagot, telling him of what was happening in London:

Certayne of our marchantes in June last sent one Captayne Furbusher with 2 shypes and a pinesse [a light sailing ship] to syke the Land of Cathay where ye Portingalles also trade, . . . our men say the[y] have brought a mann of the country with them and a bote; th[y] toke him b[y] force; he eateth raw fleshe; our men have lost a bote and v men.

5   Gerrit de Veer (fl. 1600)
Warhafftige Relation der dreyen newen
unerhörten seltzamen Schiffart . . .

    Nuremberg, Levinus Hulsius, 1598
    Shelf mark: G 690 1594 V4 G4 1598 Cage
    The Gift of Evelyn Stefannson Nef

In 1577 Frobisher returned to Baffin Island. On July 19, a member of Frobisher's crew captured an Eskimo man. On August 2, they captured a young woman and a child. The captives arrived in Bristol, England, in early October and attracted considerable attention. The man paddled his kayak on the river Avon, killing two ducks with his dart.

The "wild man" seen in Bristol is depicted in this hand-colored woodcut, one of many surviving pictures of these Eskimos. Like other such illustrations (and descriptive texts), it contains details recorded with varying degrees of accuracy. The tent in the background is European, a detail supplied by an artist who did not have an opportunity to see a real Eskimo tent. He must, however, have seen an Eskimo use a bird dart, for the method of using the dart and its throwing board (the part held by the Eskimo) is accurately shown.

6   Charles de Rochefort (b. 1605)
     The History of Barbados . . . And the rest of the
     Caribby-Islands . . . Englished by J. Davies
         London, for Thomas Starkey and Thomas
         Dring, Junr., 1666
         Shelf mark: R 1739

Charles de Rochefort interrupted his history of the
Caribbean islands, published in French in 1658, to
describe Eskimo garments brought back from
Davis Strait by the captain of a Dutch ship. De
Rochefort tells his readers that the engraver has
represented the coat and outer garments so well
that he, de Rochefort, need not elaborate. Among
the items the ship brought from the Baffin Bay
area were suits of clothes "whereof some were
of the skins of beasts, others of those of birds,
. . . shirts . . . caps, gloves, buskins, quivers,
arrows, bows, and other arms . . . some of their
tents, bags, baskets . . . [and] their boats." Some
of these objects were probably displayed on board
ship or at dockside before they made their way into
private collections.

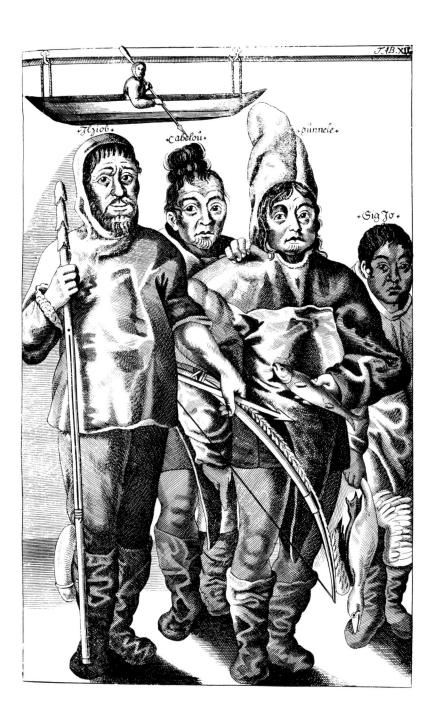

7   *Museum Regium seu Catalogus Rerum tam*
     naturalium, quam artificialium, quae in
     Basilica Bibliothecae . . . Daniae Norvegiaq;
     Monarchae Christiani Quinti . . . Descriptus
     Ab Oligero Jacobaeo

        Copenhagen, Joachim Schmetgen, 1696
        Shelf mark: AM 101 C7 1696 Cage

Four Eskimos from Greenland, captured by a
Danish expedition in 1654, were taken to Bergen,
Norway, where their portrait was painted. The
unknown artist has quite skillfully reproduced
their features, clothing, and implements for hunting and fishing. The painting was added to the
Danish royal *kunstkammer*, or museum, and is
reproduced in this catalogue of the museum collection published in 1696.

Mapping a New World

For Europeans, the "discovery" of America was more than just the finding of a new land. It was an event that provoked uncertainty about long-held beliefs. People gradually realized that the world was far larger and composed of more lands than they had imagined. It took almost a generation for Europeans to be confident that America was not simply an appendage of the Asian continent and to understand that what was at first believed to be a few islands was, in fact, a previously unknown "4th part of the world." Decades of errors and improvements in mapping were to pass before most people could begin to envision the revised shape of the world. Only after several centuries of careful work, largely by Dutch and German geographers, did a truly accurate cartographic image of America evolve.

8   Hartmann Schedel (1440–1514)
Liber Chronicarum
    Augsburg, Johann Schönsperger, 1497
    Shelf mark: INC S282

Hartmann Schedel's world map in the *Nuremberg Chronicle* was copied from Pomponius Mela and shows the world as it was known to Ptolemy and the ancients. Divided into three continents, Africa, Asia, and Europe, it is held up by Noah's three sons, Ham, Shem, and Japheth, who, according to the Bible, colonized the world after the flood. Jerusalem is located at the center of the world. Numerous mythological creatures, described in medieval travel tales, were believed to inhabit the outskirts of the world and were often pictured in the borders of maps.

9   Peter Apian (1495–1552)

Cosmographia

Antwerp, Gregorio Bontio, 1550
Shelf mark: GA 6 A7 1550 Cage

From 1544 onward, many editions of the *Cos-mographia* of the mathematician Peter Apian feature his heart-shaped world map on which America appears as a long continent rather than the group of islands described by the first explorers. North America, named "Baccalearum" from Newfound-land's name for the codfish, is shown as a slim peninsula stretching from east to west, whereas South America, drawn more accurately, bears references to the "Canibales" in Brazil and the region of the giants. Mythological elements still appear on the map itself and in its border.

10   Sebastian Münster (1489–1552)
      Cosmographiae universalis
          Basel, Heinrich Petri, 1554
          Shelf mark: G 113 M7 1554 Cage

On this map, America still appears as large islands, much as it did on maps printed earlier in the 16th century. Florida and Labrador are divided by a large sound, while Newfoundland is drawn as a long extension of Scandinavia. The west coast of Central America appears at the right of the map, labeled "Temistitan," a distortion of "Tenochtitlán," the Aztec name of Mexico City. South America also keeps the island shape, suggested by its name "Brasilia Insula." Although it is reminiscent of the Ptolemaic tradition, this map also features new geographical elements: the Pacific Ocean is named, and unidentified islands have been drawn in the general vicinity of Australia.

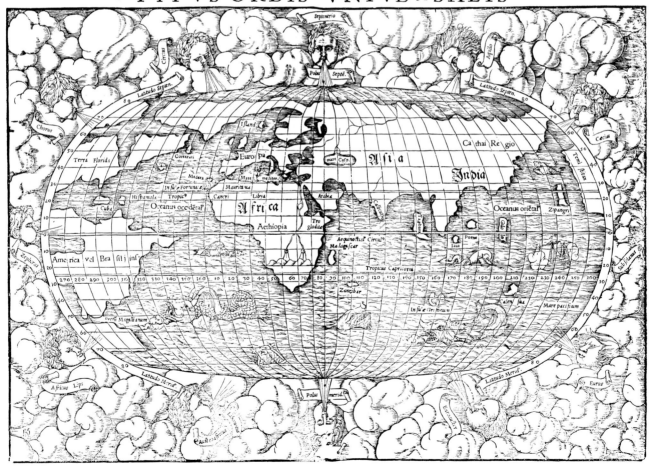

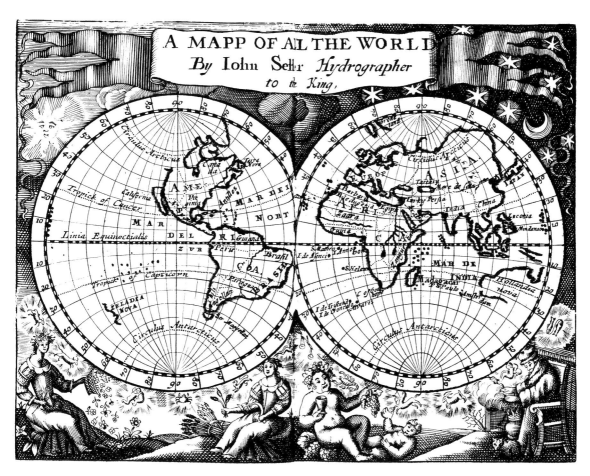

11   John Seller (fl. 1700)
      Atlas Minimus; or, A Book of Geography
      [London, sold by John Seller, 1679]
      Shelf mark: S 2465

By the second half of the 17th century, world maps reflected vast improvements in the sciences of geography and cartography. This one provides accurate coastal delineation of the continents, and half the map is devoted to the representation of lands explored by Europeans over the preceding 200 years, with space left for future discoveries. It reflects a more scientific approach, one that recognizes the limits of current knowledge. Although most of America is completed, the coasts of Alaska are left unfinished, and California remains an island. In the Pacific Ocean, only part of Australia and the east coast of New Zealand are clearly drawn. Even though this is an English map, many of the geographical names in the New World are given in Spanish (or near-Spanish), while most of the rest are in Latin.

"All His Apparell, Behaviour, and Gesture Were Very Strange to the Beholders"

Richard Hakluyt, *Principall Navigations*, 1589

The majority of the Native Americans taken back to Europe in the 16th century were probably Brazilian. Richard Hakluyt (1552?–1616) described the appearance and behavior of a "savage king" from Brazil seen at the English court in 1530:

> One of the savage kings of the Countrey of Brasill was contented to take shippe with him, and to be transported hither into England: . . . This Brasilian king being arrived, was brought up to London, and presented to king Henry the 8, lying as then at Whitehall: at the sight of whome, the king and all the Nobilitie did not a little marveile, and not withoute cause; for in his cheekes were holes made according to their savage manner, and therein small bones were planted, standing an inche out from the said holes, which in his owne Countrey was reputed for a great braverie. He had also another hole in his nether lippe, wherein was set a precious stone about the bignesse of a pearle: All his apparell, behaviour, and gesture were very strange to the beholders.

Tupinamba Indians, like the one described by Hakluyt, could be seen in a number of cities on the Continent and in a few instances took part in public festivities. As a result, some quite accurate depictions of the Tupinamba appeared in print. The French essayist Michel Eyquem de Montaigne compared the behavior of the Brazilians to that of his countrymen in his famous essay, "Des cannibales" (see cat. no. 15).

Icon Regis Quoniambec.

Rex apud Cannibales .

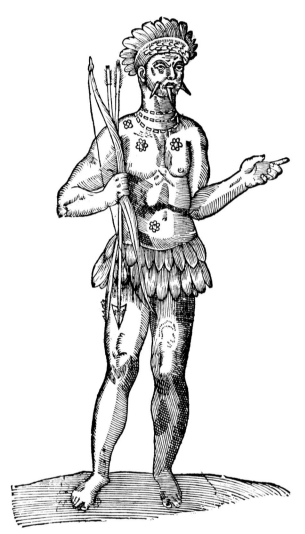

12 Ulisse Aldrovandi (1522–1605?)
Monstrorum Historia
 Bologna, Nicolo Tebaldini, 1642
 Shelf mark: ac 167114

The Italian naturalist Ulisse Aldrovandi founded a museum in Bologna to house his vast collection of materials from around the world, and hired artists to draw and paint specimens for him. His goal was to catalogue and describe the entire natural world. He published a number of books intended to be part of an extensive natural history, and after his death, his students compiled other volumes from his manuscripts. His *Monstrorum Historia*, published 37 years after his death, includes illustrations of two Brazilian men, one of whom is adorned with bones in the manner described by Hakluyt. The representation of their feather apparel and their implements is fairly accurate; Aldrovandi's artist probably worked from life. The word *monster* in the title of this work means something extraordinary or unnatural, a marvel.

ÆTATIS HABITVS. 36

D 4

13   Jacobus Sluperius (1532–1602)
      Omnium Fere Gentium nostraeque aetatis
      Nationum, Habitus & Effigies
         Antwerp, Jean Bellère, 1572
         Shelf mark: GT 513 S6 1572 Cage

Costume books and compilations of the customs
and beliefs of other cultures appeared in numerous
editions in the second half of the 16th and
throughout the 17th century. Some were more
scholarly than others, but most were serious
attempts to collect and distribute information
about the dress and behavior of people in other
parts of the world. The Brazilian man illustrated
here is a Tupinamba. The large feather rosette, or
bustle, the knife hung around his neck, the feather
head ornament, and the bow and arrows agree
with what present-day ethnographers know about
Tupinamba dress and weapons.

14   Jean de Léry (1534–1611)
      Historia Navigationis In Brasiliam
         [Geneva], Eustathius Vignon, 1586
         Shelf mark: F 2511 L6 L2 Cage

Jean de Léry spent most of the year 1557 in Brazil.
His account of that visit, first published in 1578,
contains five realistic woodcuts of Tupinamba
Indians. This one, of an Indian couple and child,
includes a good representation of their hammock
and illustrates the sling used by women to carry
their infants. The man has an ornament, possibly a
pearl, in his lower lip.

15 Michel Eyquem de Montaigne (1533–1592)
"Of the Caniballes," from *The Essayes*
. . . done into English by . . . John Florio

London, Val. Sims for Edward Blount, 1603
Shelf mark: STC 18041 cop. 2

Montaigne's famous essay was probably written after he saw Tupinamba Indians in Rouen, but it deals as much with the citizens of his native France as it does with the Indians. He describes the "cannibals" as inhabitants of an earthly paradise from which they have not fallen, unlike the rest of humankind, an argument which contributed greatly to the myth of the Noble Savage. Obsessed with the cruelty of the religious wars in his own country, Montaigne overlooks the cruelty of some Indian customs and describes the Brazilians as much less barbarous than the French, "unlesse men call that barbarisme which is not common to them." With a reference to the Brazilians' nudity, Montaigne sarcastically condemns the prejudices of his countrymen who judge other people on their appearance: "All that is not very ill; but what of that? They weare no kind of breeches or hosen."

The thirtieth Chapter.

Of the Caniballes.

AT what time King *Pirrhus* came into *Italie*, after he had furvaide the marfhalling of the Armie, which the Romaines fent againft him : *I wot not,* faid he, *what barbarous men thefe are* (for fo were the Græcians wont to call all ftrange nations) *but the difpofition of this Armie, which I fee, is nothing barbarous.* So faid the Græcians of that which *Flaminius* fent into their countrie : And *Phillip* viewing from a Tower the order and diftribution of the Romaine campe, in his kingdome, vnder *Publius Sulpitius Galba .* Loe how a man ought to take heede, left he over-weeningly follow vulgar opinions, which fhould be meafured by the rule of reafon, and not by the common report. I have had long time dwelling with mee a man, who for the fpace of tenne or twelve yeares had dwelt in that other world, which in our age was lately difcovered in thofe partes where *Villegaignon* firft landed, and furnamed *Antartike France.* This difcoverie of fo infinite and vaft a countrie, feemeth worthie great confideration. I wot not whether I can warrant my felfe, that fome other be not difcovered hereafter, fithence fo many worthie men, and better learned then we are, have fo many ages beene deceived in this. I feare me our eyes be greater then our bellies, and that we have more curiofitie then capacitie. We embrace all, but we faften nothing but winde. *Plato* maketh *Solon* to reporte, that he had learn't of the Priefts of the Cittie of *Says* in *Ægypt*, that whilom, and before the generall Deluge, there was a great Iland called *Atlantides*, fituated at the mouth of the ftraite of *Gibralterre*, which contained more firme land then *Affrike* and *Afia* together. And that the Kings of that countrie, who did not onely poffeffe that Iland, but had fo farre entred into the maine-land, that of the breadth of *Affrike* , they held as farre as *Ægypt*; and of *Europes* length, as farre as *Tufcanie*: and that they vndertooke to invade *Afia*, and to fubdue all the nations that compaffe the Mediterranean Sea, to the gulfe of *Mare-Maggiore*, and to that end they traverfed all *Spaine, France* and *Italie*, fo farre as *Greece*, where the Athenians made head againft them ; but that a while after, both the Athenians themfelves, and that great Iland, were fwallowed vp by the Deluge. It is very likely this extreame ruine of waters wrought ftrange alterations in the habitations of the earth : as fome holde that the Sea hath divided *Sicilie* from *Italie*,

Virg. Aen. lib. 3
414. 416.

> *Hæc loca vi quondam, & vafta convulfa ruina*
> *Diffiluiffe ferunt, cùm protinus vtraque tellus*
> *Vna foret.*
> Men fay, fometimes this land by that forfaken,
> And that by this, were fplit, and ruine-fhaken,
> Whereas till then both lands as one were taken.

Cypres from *Soria*, the Iland of *Negroponte* from the maine land of *Beotia* , and in other places joyned landes that were fundred by the Sea, filling with mudde and fand the chanels betweene them.

Hor. art. Poet.
65.

> —*fterilifque diu palus aptáque remis*
> *Vicinas vrbes alit, & grave fentit aratrum.*
> The fenne long barren, to be row'd in, nowe
> Both feedes the neighbour townes, and feeles the plowe.

But there is no great apparance, the faid Iland fhould be the new world we have lately difcovered ; for, it well-nigh touched *Spaine*, and it were an incredible effect of inundation,

ſo

"The True Pictures and Fashions of the People in . . . Virginia"

Thomas Harriot, *A briefe and true report*, 1590

Little is known about the artist John White, who was part of Sir Walter Raleigh's 1585–1586 expedition to what is now coastal North Carolina. We do know that he worked with another member of that expedition, Thomas Harriot, who was a mathematician and cartographer. Together they mapped the area of Roanoke Island and recorded information on the native population and natural resources. White made field sketches in America in 1585–1586 and again in 1587 and produced finished versions when he returned to England. The field sketches have not survived, but the finished watercolors, now in the collection of the British Museum, are among the most important and accurate 16th-century illustrations of American Indians and their way of life.

White's depictions of the Algonquian Indians would not have had a major impact on European images of the inhabitants of North America if they had not been copied by the engraver Theodor de Bry. The drawings themselves were seen by a relatively small number of people, but de Bry's engravings, which were published with the text of Harriot's *A briefe and true report . . . of Virginia* as the first part of de Bry's *Grands Voyages*, distributed these images to a wide audience. German, French, and Latin editions, as well as a special English edition dedicated to Sir Walter Raleigh, were published in 1590. Most subsequent 17th-century images of eastern North American Indians were based on those by de Bry.

16   John White (fl. 1585–1593)
A Cheife Herowans Wyfe of Pomeoc and her
Daughter of the Age of 8 or 10 Yeares
        Reproduction of watercolor drawing courtesy
        of the Trustees of the British Museum

White's drawings preserve valuable information on
perishable items such as wood, fur, and leather,
which generally have not survived for study by
archaeologists and ethnographers. The drawings
also illustrate the ways in which the Algonquians
decorated their bodies with tattooing and body
paint, as can be seen on the woman in this drawing; she also wears a skirt made of fringed skin. In
contrast, the girl holds a doll that is clothed in an
Elizabethan-style dress.

17   John White (fl. 1585–1593)
Indians Dancing
> Reproduction of watercolor drawing courtesy
> of the Trustees of the British Museum

According to Thomas Harriot, the dance shown in this drawing was held at night "at a Certayne tyme of the yere . . . every man attyred in the most strange fashion they can devise." He described the posts around which the Indians dance as "carved with heads like to the faces of Nonnes covered with theyr vayls."

Theire sitting at meate .

18   John White (fl. 1585–1593)
      Theire Sitting at Meate
         Reproduction of watercolor drawing courtesy
         of the Trustees of the British Museum

Aside from illustrating the manner in which an
Algonquian couple would eat a meal, White's
watercolor contains many details of body decoration and dress, such as the man's ear ornament and
hairstyle, the paint on his face and forehead, his
fringed deerskin mantle, the woman's skin robe,
and her necklace of beads or pearls.

19   John White (fl. 1585–1593)
      The Manner of their Attire and Painting
      Themselves when they goe to their generall
      Huntings, or at theire Solemne Feasts
          Reproduction of watercolor drawing courtesy
          of the Trustees of the British Museum

This drawing shows not only elaborate body painting but also the fringed deerskin apron-skirts worn
by many of the Algonquian men, complete with a
long tail (possibly of a puma) at the back. The man
also wears a wrist guard of skin and feather ornaments in his hair.

A weroan or great Lorde of Virginia. III.

THe Princes of Virginia are attyred in suche manner as is expressed in this figure.
They weare the haire of their heades long and bynde opp the ende of thesame in
a knot vnder thier eares. Yet they cutt the topp of their heades from the forehead
to the nape of the necke in manner of a cokscombe, stirkinge a faier lõge pecher of
some berd att the Beginge of the creste vppun their foreheads, and another short
one on bothe seides about their eares. They hange at their eares ether thicke pearles,
or somwhat els, as the clawe of some great birde, as cometh in to their fansye. Moreouer They
ether pownes, or paynt their forehead, cheeks, chynne, bodye, armes, and leggs, yet in another sorte
then the inhabitantz of Florida. They weare a chaine about their necks of pearles or beades of copper, wich they muche esteeme, and ther of wear they also braselets ohn their armes. Vnder their
bresbs about their bellyes appeir certayne spotts, whear they vse to lett them selues bloode, when they
are sicke. They hange before thẽ the skinne of some beaste verye feinelye dresset in suche sorte, that
the tayle hangeth downe behynde. They carye a quiuer made of small rushes holding their bowe
readie bent in on hand, and an arrowe in the other, radie to defend themselues. In this manner they
goe to warr, or tho their solemne feasts and banquetts. They take muche pleasure in huntinge of
deer wher of theris great store in the contrye, for yt is fruit full, pleasant, and full of Goodly woods. Yt
hathe also store of riuers full of diuers sorts of fishe. When they go to battel they paynt their bo-
dyes in the most terible manner that thei can deuise.

20   Thomas Harriot (1560–1621)

A briefe and true report of the new found land of Virginia

Frankfurt, Johann Wechel for Theodor de Bry, 1590
Shelf mark: STC 12786

De Bry's engraving entitled *A weroan or great Lorde of Virginia* is based on White's drawing of an Indian man in elaborate body paint (cat. no. 19). Alterations made by the engraver are obvious. He has shown the figure in reverse and has added a rear view of him, as well as a background of other Indians hunting with bows and arrows. There are also minor variations in the earrings and patterns in the body paint on the legs. *Their sitting at meate* has also been modified from the White drawing (cat. no. 18). Some background has been added, additional objects are shown on the mat, and the postures of the man and woman have been altered.

Mulier Virginiæ insulæ Habitatrix.

Vir Virginiæ insulæ Habitator.

21   Pietro Bertelli (fl. 1580–1616)
Diversarum Nationum Habitus
   Padua, Alciatus Alcia and Pietro Bertelli,
   1594–1596
   Shelf mark: GT 513 B4 Cage

Although Theodor de Bry modified John White's drawings to some extent, he followed them quite faithfully when depicting clothing and artifacts. Postures and body types were likely to be altered, however, when de Bry and other artists followed traditional European models. Almost as soon as the de Bry engravings were published, other artists began to copy them. Pietro Bertelli's book, on the costume of various nations, appeared only a few years after de Bry's publication of the White illustrations. His woman and man of Virginia (above) are crudely copied from the title page of de Bry's edition of Harriot (left), and the backgrounds come from other de Bry engravings.

John Smith (1580–1631)

The Generall Historie of Virginia

London, by I. D. and I. H. for Michael
Sparkes, 1624
Shelf mark: STC 22790

Robert Vaughan, the artist who engraved this plate illustrating some of the adventures of Captain John Smith, also clearly derived most of his material from de Bry's engravings. The king of Pamaunkee being taken prisoner by Smith in the upper right corner of the plate is a close copy of the "weroan or great lorde of Virginia" in Harriot. The figures of the conjurer, the idol, and the priest at upper center are derived from de Bry, as is the dance scene on the left. The feather headdresses worn by King Powhatan and the idol, however, are not found in de Bry.

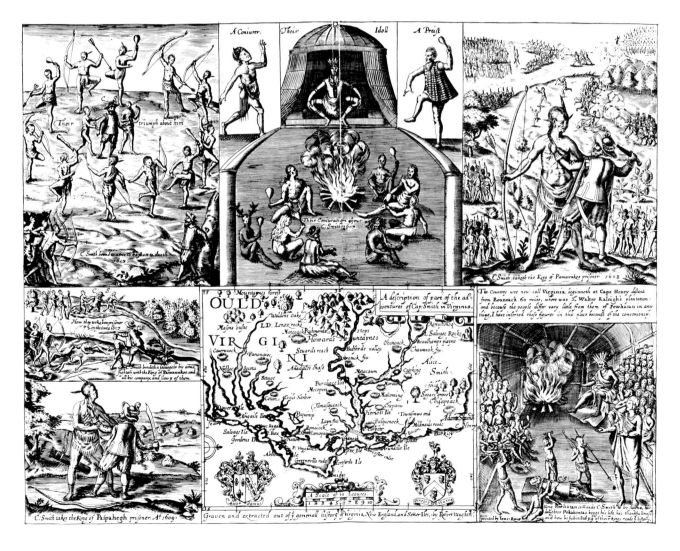

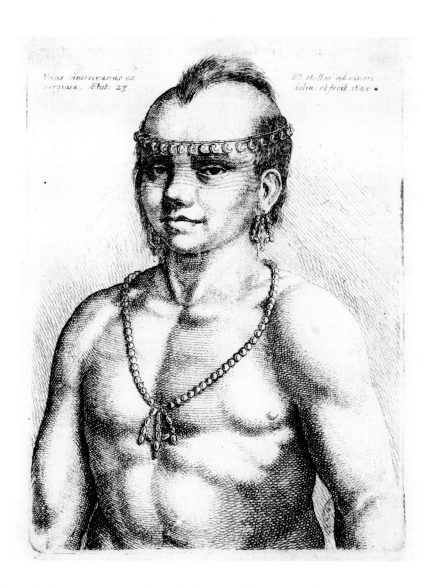

23   Wenceslaus Hollar (1607–1677)

Unus Americanus ex Virginia

[Antwerp], 1645
Shelf mark: Art Box H737.5 no. 29
The Gift of Barbara Fahs Charles

One of the few 17th-century illustrations of a Virginia Indian not based on de Bry is this engraving by the Czech artist Wenceslaus Hollar. Hollar's model has been recently identified by scholars George F. Hamell and Christian F. Feest as a Munsee Delaware man known as Jacques who, in 1644, was taken from New Amsterdam to Amsterdam. Hollar was in Amsterdam in 1645 and would have seen the Indian at that time. It was not unusual to refer to New Netherland as "Virginia" in this period.

"There Was No Talke, No Hope, No Worke, but Dig Gold, Wash Gold, Refine Gold, Loade Gold"

Captain John Smith, *The Generall Historie of Virginia*, Book III, 1624

Europeans had long heard tales of the gold to be found in Guinea and the riches of the East. Like the 15th-century explorers of Africa, Columbus and those who followed him to the New World were influenced by these tales and determined to find gold in the newly discovered "Indies."

When Cortés landed in Mexico in 1519, the emperor Montezuma presented him with precious gifts, which Cortés sent to his own emperor, Charles V. These treasures were displayed in Seville, Valladolid, and Brussels. The artist Albrecht Dürer saw them in Brussels in 1520 and wrote in his diary: "I have also seen the things brought to the king from the new golden land: a sun all of gold a whole fathom broad, also a moon all of silver."

Tales of such precious objects and an influx of silver and gold from mines in Peru and Mexico contributed to a growing European obsession with the riches of the New World. The myth of the city of El Dorado, paved with gold, and of its chief, covered in gold, drove many expeditions of Spanish, German, and English explorers to distant regions in South America, including Venezuela, Guiana, Columbia, and Brazil. The ruthless pursuit of New World riches led to atrocities against the natives, atrocities that were gradually documented in print.

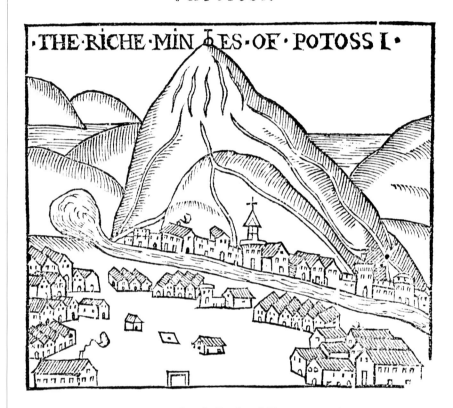

THE
DISCOVERIE AND CONQVEST
of the Prouinces of *PERV,* and
the Nauigation in the South
Sea, along that Coaſt.
And alſo of the ritche Mines
of *POTOSI.*

·THE·RICHE·MIN ΔES·OF·POTOSS I·

Imprinted at London by Richard Ihones. *Febru.6.1581.*

24   Augustín de Zárate (b. 1514)
      *The . . . History of the discoverie and Conquest
      of . . . Peru*
        London, Richard Jhones, 1581
        Shelf mark: STC 26123

The discovery of the Potosí silver mines in 1540 drew many immigrants to Peru. Augustín de Zárate traveled there in 1543 and, while serving as an accountant to the emperor, witnessed the Spanish quarrels over the division of Potosí's riches. Zárate's history of the conquest of Peru, first printed in 1555, served as an advertisement of New World riches. Descriptions of Spanish greed in this English translation may have contributed to anti-Spanish sentiment in England.

25 Sir Walter Raleigh (1552?–1618)
    The Discoverie Of The . . . Empire Of Guiana
       London, Robert Robinson, 1596
       Shelf mark: STC 20634

Sir Walter Raleigh was among those who searched in vain for the city of gold "which the *Spaniards* cal *El Dorado*, that for the greatnes, for the riches, and for the excellent seate, it farre exceedeth any of the world." This account of Raleigh's 1595 expedition to Guiana perpetuated the El Dorado myth. Raleigh's enthusiasm led him twice to search for the fabled city, in spite of the previous failure of many Spanish and German expeditions. Raleigh was also driven by his belief that Spain's growing power would be curtailed if England cut off her supply of gold and silver from the New World. After his final, hopeless voyage in 1617, he returned to England in disgrace.

THE
DISCOVERIE
OF THE LARGE,
RICH, AND BEVVTIFVL
EMPIRE OF GVIANA, WITH
a relation of the great and Golden Citie
of Manoa (which the spanyards call El
Dorado) And the Prouinces of *Emeria*,
Arromaia, Amapaia, and other Coun-
tries, with their riuers, ad-
ioyning.

Performed in the yeare 1595. by Sir
W. Ralegh Knight, Captaine of her
Maiesties Guard, Lo. Warden
of the Stinneries, and her High-
nesse Lieutenant generall
of the Countie of
Cornewall.

Imprinted at London by Robert Robinson.
1596.

Sir Francis Drake Reuiued :

Calling vpon this Dull or Effeminate Age, to follow his Noble steps for Gold and Siluer.

By this Memorable Relation, of the Rare occurrences (neuer yet declared to the World) in a third Voyage, made by him into the West-Indies, in the yeeres 72. and 73. when *Nombre de Dios* was by him and fiftie two others onely in his Companie surprised.

Faithfully taken out of the Report of M. *Christopher Ceely*, *Ellis Hixom*, and others, who were in the same Voyage with him.

By PHILIP NICHOLS, Preacher.

Reuiewed by Sir FRANCIS DRAKE himselfe before his death, and much holpen and enlarged by diuers Notes, with his owne hand here and there Inserted.

Set forth by Sir FRANCIS DRAK'E Baronet (his Nephew) now liuing.

AVXILIO DIVINO

SIC PARVIS MAGNA

LONDON,
Printed for *Nicholas Bourne*, dwelling at the South Entrance of the Royall Exchange, 1 6 2 8.

26   Philip Nichols

Sir Francis Drake Revived: Calling upon this Dull or Effeminate Age, to follow his Noble steps for Gold and Silver

London, for Nicholas Bourne, 1628
Shelf mark: STC 18545

English activity in the Caribbean began around 1562, as did their harassment of the Spanish there. Years later, as the legend of El Dorado faded, Philip Nichols revived the story of Sir Francis Drake's successful voyage to Panama in 1572–1573 when he fought the Spanish and came away with gold, silver, and pearls.

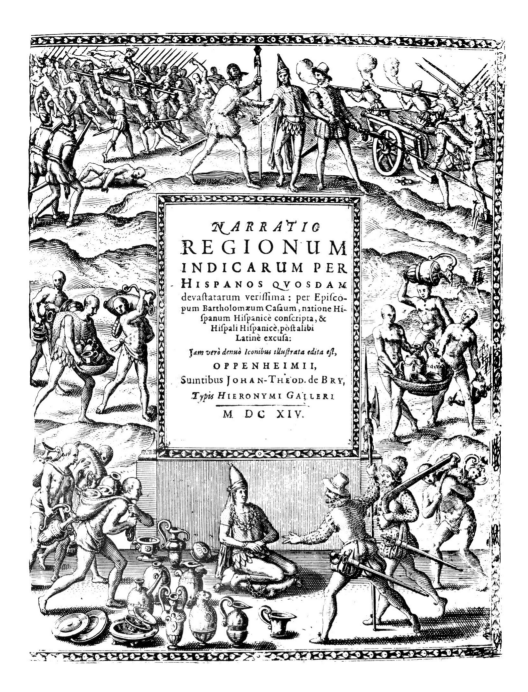

NARRATIO
REGIONUM
INDICARUM PER
HISPANOS QVOSDAM
devaſtatarum veriſſima : per Epiſco-
pum Bartholomæum Caſaum, natione Hí-
ſpanum Hiſpanicè conſcripta, &
Hiſpali Hiſpanicè, poſt alibi
Latinè excuſa:
Jam verò denuò Iconibus illuſtrata edita eſt,
OPPENHEIMII,
Sumtibus JOHAN-THEOD. de BRY,
Typis HIERONYMI GALLERI
M DC XIV.

27   Bartolomé de Las Casas (1474–1566)
     *Narratio Regionum Indicarum Per Hispanos
     quosdam devastatarum verissima*

     Oppenheim, Johann Theodor de Bry, 1614
     Shelf mark: F 1411 C2 L2 1614 Cage

The writings of Bartolomé de Las Casas decrying the oppression and exploitation of Native Americans by his fellow Spaniards were influential, widely read, and controversial. A Dominican friar and the future bishop of Chiapas, Las Casas exposed the greed for gold behind the Spanish conquest of New World lands. This work, first published in Seville in 1552 as *Brevissima relación de la destruyción de las Indias*, was his most famous and contributed greatly to the so-called Black Legend of Spanish cruelty and to the decline of Spain's reputation in Europe. Engravings by the de Bry family in this Latin edition illustrate torture of the natives and the plundering of their gold and other possessions.

28   Theodor de Bry (1528–1598)

America Pars Quarta . . . Scripta ab Hieronymo Benzono

     Frankfurt, Johann Feyerabend, 1594
     Shelf mark: G 159 B7 1590 v.2 Cage

The series of engravings and texts depicting the New World produced by Theodor de Bry and his family was a monumental undertaking published in 13 parts over a period of 44 years. De Bry, a Protestant from Liège, had observed the success with which Flemish printers had used engravings to further Catholic propaganda. The engravings produced by the de Bry family for their series, known as the *Grands Voyages*, had an equally powerful effect, publicizing and promoting the exploration and colonization of the New World

while condemning cruelty to and exploitation of the native peoples. This illustration from part 4, a translation of Girolamo Benzoni's history of the New World, is based on a crude woodcut in the 1565 edition of Benzoni and shows the Indians taking revenge on the Spanish thirst for gold by pouring molten gold into the Spaniards' mouths. Although the Indians in the background appear as cannibals and the punishment they inflict seems savage, the engraving is essentially critical of the Spanish and sympathetic to native rebellion. No evidence survives as to whether the Indians actually carried out this form of revenge; perhaps de Bry simply used this illustration as potent propaganda.

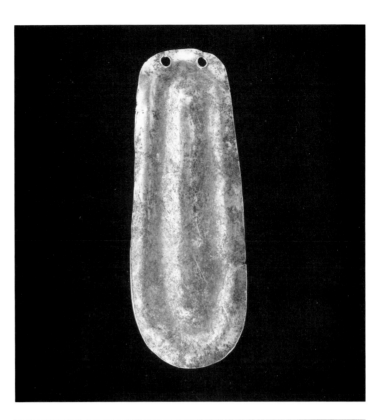

29 Jaguar necklace pendant *(above)*
    Cast gold, l. 3.5 cm
    From a mound in the northeastern
    Everglades
    Lent by the Department of Anthropology,
    National Museum of Natural History,
    Smithsonian Institution, no. 391062

30 Necklace pendant *(top right)*
    Hammered gold (or gold-copper alloy),
    l. 5.5 cm
    From a mound on Cape Canaveral
    Lent by the Department of Anthropology,
    National Museum of Natural History,
    Smithsonian Institution, no. 385364

31 Disc, perhaps for a breast or ear ornament
    (bottom right)
        Hammered gold (or gold-copper alloy),
        diam. 7.3 cm
        From a mound in the northern Everglades
        Lent by the Department of Anthropology,
        National Museum of Natural History,
        Smithsonian Institution, no. 340747

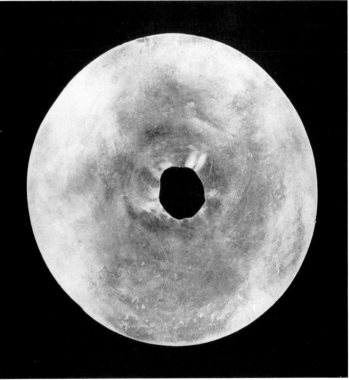

Very few gold or silver objects of Indian manufac-
ture collected by the Spanish in the 16th and 17th
centuries escaped the melting pot. These three are
in the style of the Quimbaya region of south-
western Colombia. Found in archaeological sites
in southern Florida, they were undoubtedly recov-
ered by Indians from ships of the Spanish plate
fleets that were wrecked off the southeast coast of
Florida.

"The Very Proportion of an Armed Horse"

Roger Barlow, *A Brief Summe of Geographie*, c. 1540

Many of the birds and animals of America seemed as exotic to the Europeans as the people and artifacts seen in and brought back from the New World. Columbus remarked on the continuous singing of "nightingales" and the brilliant plumage of parrots. Among the animals, the armadillo attracted great attention. Roger Barlow tried to describe it, calling it a small beast no bigger than a baby pig but with the feet, head, and ears of a horse, concluding that "it is the very proportion of an armed horse." Armadillo shells could be easily preserved and transported and were soon in many collections of curiosities.

Throughout the 16th and 17th centuries New World animals and birds, both live and as skinned and sometimes stuffed examples, made their way back to Europe. These were often displayed in taverns and at fairs, but specimens were also collected by zoologists for serious study. Some of the famous "wonder cabinets," or early museums, such as those of Ole Worm in Denmark and Ferrante Imperato and Ulisse Aldrovandi in Italy, contained many examples of American birds and animals. Zoological works were increasingly based on direct observation of either well-preserved specimens or animals in their natural habitats, and the exotic creatures of the New World were included and described in some detail.

DES OYSEAVX, PAR P. BELON.

Pſittaki, & Pſittacos en Grec, Pſittace, & Pſittacus en Latin, grand Papegaut en Françoys.

32 Pierre Belon (1517?–1564)
   L'Histoire de la Nature des Oyseaux
      Paris, Gilles Corrozet, 1555
      Shelf mark: QL 673 B4 1555 Cage

Pierre Belon, along with Conrad Gesner, is considered one of the founders of modern natural history and is particularly noted for his studies of anatomy. Although he traveled widely, he never visited the Americas. Since illustrations in his study *The History of the Nature of Birds* are thought to have been drawn from life, Belon must have depended on specimens brought back to Europe. African parrots had been known in Europe for some time, but those from the New World were more colorful—and they "talked." This woodcut of a parrot is certainly accurate, but Belon was as confused as many other Europeans about changing world geography. He says that parrots come from Brazil but goes on to say that the ancients named "India that which we now call Brazil."

ARMADILLO fiue AIATOCHTLI.

ARMADILLO CLVSII.

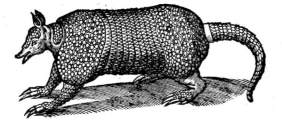

ARMADILLO GENVS ALTERVM CLVSII.

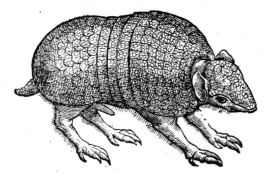

33   Juan Eusebio Nieremberg (1595–1658)
Historia Naturae Maxime Peregrinae,
Libris XVI Distincta

Antwerp, Balthasar Moretus, 1635
Shelf mark: QH 41 N6 1635 Cage

A classic of American natural history, Nieremberg's work is concerned primarily with the natural history of Mexico. The author, a Jesuit who taught natural history at the University of Madrid, described a variety of animals, plants, and minerals, setting down many of their native names in print for the first time. The work is largely derivative, and Nieremberg may have extracted some of his information from the manuscripts of Francisco Hernández, a physician who had been sent to Mexico in 1570 by Philip II to study medicinal plants. After seven years in Mexico, Hernández presented to the king 20 volumes of notes on the natural history of the country. Although none of Hernández's work was published in his lifetime, his manuscripts were placed in the library of the royal monastery in the Escorial, where Nieremberg may have seen them.

34   Willem Piso (1611–1678)
      Historia Naturalis Brasiliae
          Leiden, Franciscus Hackius; Amsterdam,
          Ludovicus Elzevir, 1648
          Shelf mark (temp.): Massey 53f
          The Gift of Mary P. Massey

In 1637 a semiscientific expedition sponsored by
the Dutch West India Company started out for
Brazil accompanied by the physician Willem Piso
and later joined by Georg Marggraf. Although
Marggraf fell ill and died in 1644, Piso returned to
the Netherlands with their manuscripts and published their work in 1648. Four sections of the
book by Piso are concerned with medicine and the
medicinal plants of northern Brazil; the remaining
eight sections by Marggraf treat the natural history
of the area. He described in detail for the first time
many New World animals and birds, including the
opossum, the hummingbird, and, here, the llama.

35 Theodor de Bry (1528–1598)
    "Guiana," from *Americae pars VIII*
    Frankfurt, Matthaeus Becker, 1599
    Shelf mark: G 159 B7 1590 v. 3 Cage

Although some very accurate illustrations and descriptions of New World fauna were in print by the second half of the 16th century, tales of strange mythological creatures found in America were still common. Most were merely extensions of medieval travelers' tales, but they were perpetuated by explorers such as Columbus and Sir Walter Raleigh.

This map of Guiana was published by the de Bry family to accompany Raleigh's account of his travels there. Authentic animals like the armadillo appear on the map, but so do a man with his head beneath his shoulders and an Amazon woman. Tales of the Amazons went back to classical times; a misreading of Indian customs led Europeans to believe that Amazons existed in the New World. Columbus claimed to have seen them after observing aggressive behavior among Indian women. The acephal, or headless man, had long been associated with Ethiopia, but Raleigh claimed that Indians on the upper Orinoco knew of such people, whom they called Exxaipanoma.

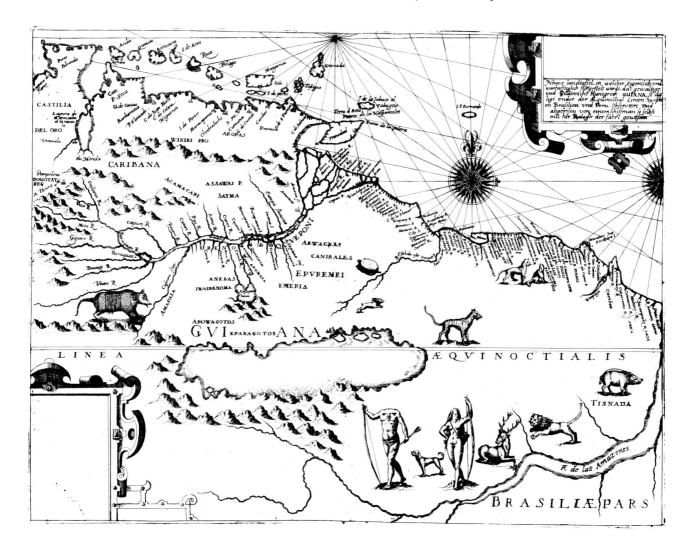

"To Search the Indies for Their Balm and Spice, Rifle the Treasure of Old Paradise"

John Rea, *Flora: seu de Florum Cultura*, 1665

The great age of the botanic garden in Europe followed the discovery of the New World. Small enclosed gardens with a variety of plants representing, or symbolically re-creating, the Garden of Eden had become popular in the early 15th century. It was uncertain whether the original garden had survived and was awaiting discovery or had been dispersed by the flood, scattering plants to the far corners of the earth. In either case, collecting and organizing plants in an attempt to re-create the original garden were activities calculated to bring the gardener closer to God.

The small enclosed garden expanded, and in the 16th century the first formal botanic gardens were established in Europe as places where the properties of plants could be studied. Many of them were associated with schools of medicine. Botanic gardens retained a symbolic purpose as well. Traditionally, they were divided into four parts representing the four corners of the earth. Gradually, however, the four parts came to represent the four continents, and plants were often laid out according to their place of origin. At first, most plants were edible or medicinal, and new ones from the Americas and other exotic parts of the world were eagerly awaited. Later, ornamental plants and trees were grown as well. By the end of the 16th century, gardeners often gave explorers lists of desired plants for their collections. By the end of the 17th century, the traveling botanist who collected plants and saw them in their natural habitat had become fairly common.

36   Leonhard Fuchs (1501–1566)
     Den Nieuwen Herbarius
        Basel, Michael Isengrin, [1550?]
        Shelf mark: QK 41 F9 D9 1550 Cage

The 16th century witnessed the publication of the great illustrated herbals. Among the most important was Leonhard Fuchs's *De Historia Stirpium*, first published in 1542. Fuchs was a physician and professor of medicine for 31 years at the University of Tübingen. Since plants for treating illness must be identified correctly, Fuchs was concerned with the accuracy of the illustrations in his herbal. He incorporated a few edible American plants in this work, including the first illustration of a maize, or corn, plant to appear in a printed book, drawn from life 50 years after Columbus had discovered it. Fuchs mistakenly identified the plant as Turkish corn, a label that appears in this Dutch translation of his book. Different varieties of maize were being grown in many European gardens at this time, which may explain some of the confusion about the plant's origins.

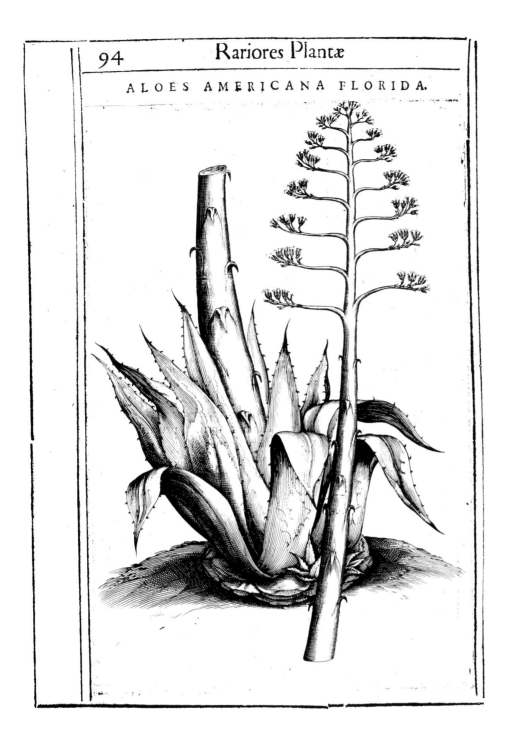

ALOES AMERICANA FLORIDA.

37   Tobia Aldini (17th cent.)
Exactissima Descriptio Rariorum Quarundam Plantarum
    Rome, Giacomo Mascardi, 1625
    Shelf mark: DG 815.5 A5 1625 Cage

In the Renaissance, plants were highly valued for their medicinal properties, and the botanic garden served as a living pharmacy. This catalogue of plants from the garden of Cardinal Farnese in Rome includes several from America, among them the aloe plant. In his introduction to the catalogue, Aldini, who was physician to the cardinal, mentions the eagerness with which he awaits plants from the New World.

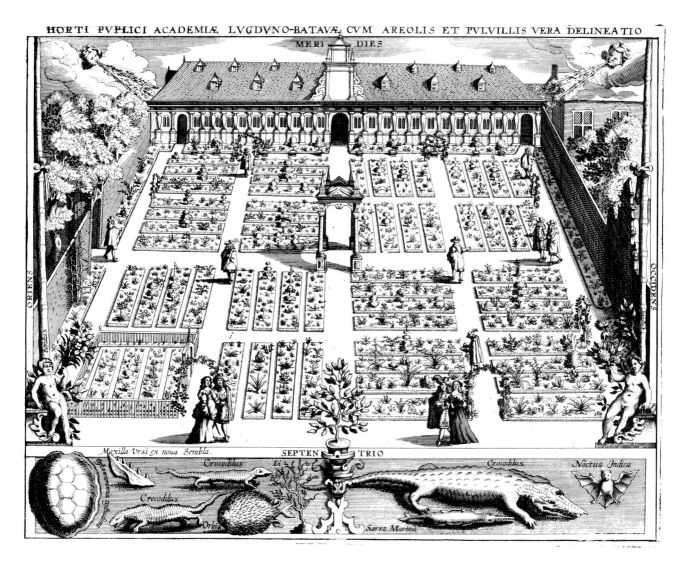

38 *Hortorum Viridariorumque Noviter in Europa*
   Engraved by Abraham Hogenberg
   [Cologne], 1655
   Shelf mark: SB 465 H6 Cage

One of the most famous botanic gardens in Europe
was established at Leiden in 1587. The garden was
laid out in the traditional four parts, and visitors were welcome to stroll its paths to see the
plants growing there. In adjacent galleries were
collections of objects such as rocks and animals,
some of which are pictured at the bottom of the
illustration.

39   Paul Hermann (1646?–1695)
      *Horti Academici Lugduno-Batavi Catalogus
      exhibens Plantarum*

          Leiden, Cornelius Boutesteyn, 1687
          Shelf mark: ac 199019

The botanic garden was organized as a living
encyclopedia of plants. Scientific classification
of plants as we know it today was formulated only
in the 18th century. Plants might be organized
in a garden according to their place of origin or
grouped according to certain properties or medicinal usage. As travel to other parts of the world
increased, more plants were introduced to botanic
gardens, including trees and ornamental plants.
This catalogue of the Leiden garden (see cat. no.
38), compiled 100 years after the garden was established, includes the Virginia tulip poplar.

"Divine Herb" and "Indian Nectar"

Tobacco and Chocolate in the New World and the Old

Stirpium Adversaria Nova (London, 1570), by Pierre Pena and Matthias de l'Obel, contained the first illustration of a tobacco plant. The accompanying illustration of the way to smoke it may have been inspired by sailors' references to "little funnels" for "drinking" its smoke.

Tobacco was probably the strangest and most exotic of the edible and medicinal plants imported to Europe from the New World. Columbus noted its use in his journal, and sailors who traveled to the New World certainly learned to chew and smoke it. English sailors referred to cigars as "little funnels," which the Indians used to "drink" tobacco smoke. References to tobacco began to appear in print early in the 16th century. The principal varieties of tobacco were grown in botanical gardens by the third quarter of the century, although they were not yet accurately classified. The first illustration of a tobacco plant appeared in a botanical work published in 1570, with reference to its curative powers for "sores, wounds, affections of the throat and chest, and the fever of the plague."

Whether tobacco was a wonder drug or a "witching weed," which drove men out of their minds and ruined their health, was debated, but the controversy did not stop Europeans from trying it. Although both Hans Staden and Jean de Léry witnessed and wrote about the Indians' use of tobacco in religious rituals and as a magical cure, these applications of the plant in the New World were little known or understood by Europeans. De Bry illustrated a Tupinamba dance ceremony in which the priests used tobacco smoke to help dancers communicate with powerful spirits.

Edmund Spenser, in *The Faerie Queene*, praised Sir Walter Raleigh for helping to introduce "divine tobacco or panachaea" to England. Viewed by some as a "divine herb" and by others as a "devilish" plant "hateful to the nose, harmful to the brain" (James I, *A Counter-blaste to Tobacco*), tobacco became a part of European life and of a new set of social rituals quite unlike those associated with its use in the New World.

The convivial atmosphere of taverns and alehouses, and later in the mid-17th century, coffeehouses, provided the ideal setting for the social habit of smoking and for the introduction of other exotic products, such as coffee from Turkey and chocolate from Mexico.

The Tupinamba ritual of the maracas (rattles) was illustrated by
Theodor de Bry in *Americae tertia pars* (Frankfurt, 1605). The smoke
blown on the dancers by the priests was believed to facilitate communication with powerful spirits enclosed in the rattles who would help
the dancers conquer their enemies.

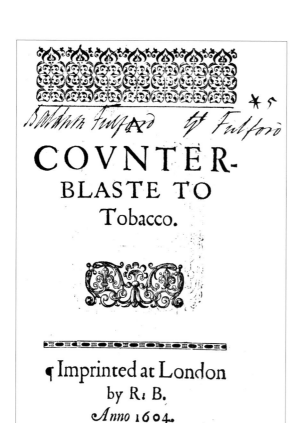

A
COVNTER-
BLASTE TO
Tobacco.

¶ Imprinted at London
by R₁ B.
Anno 1604.

Work for Chimny-sweepers:
OR
A warning for Tabacconifts.

Defcribing the pernicious
vfe of *Tabacco*, no leffe plea-
fant then profitable for all forts
to reade.

Fumus patria, Igne alieno Luculentior.

As much to fay,

Better be chokt with Englifh hemp,
then poifoned with Indian Tabacco.

Imprinted at London by T.Efte, for Thomas
Bufhell, & are to be fould at the great North
dore of Powles. 1602.

A DEFENCE OF
TABACCO: VVITH A
FRIENDLY ANSWER TO THE
late printed Booke called
Worke for Chimny-Swee-
pers, &c.

Si iudicas, cognofce : fi Rex es, iube.

LONDON,
Printed by *Richard Field* for *Thomas Man*.
1 6 0 2.

Above left: James I of England was the first European
ruler to take any official step against smoking. His
Counter-blaste to Tobacco (London, 1604) had little
effect on the popularity of tobacco and smoking.

Above: An anonymous author, who called himself
Philaretes, also wrote against tobacco in *Work for
Chimny-sweepers: or, A warning for Tabacconists* (London, 1602 [1601]). He warned against the satanic
origins of the plant.

Left: In England, Philaretes's work was the first of a
long series of polemical tracts about smoking. Roger
Marbeck answered him in *A Defence of Tabacco* (London, 1602).

This woodcut of a coffeehouse where coffee and tobacco were both enjoyed illustrates "A broadside against coffee," which was published with a 1672 edition of James I's *A Counterblast to Tobacco*. Attacks against tobacco were often also directed against other exotic pleasures, such as Turkish coffee.

Another exotic import from the New World was chocolate or cocoa. In pre-Columbian civilizations, cocoa was associated with religious rituals at the highest levels of Aztec and Mayan societies. Cocoa beans were precious and often used as money. Considered a beverage of the gods and the elite, cocoa was believed to have a special spiritual power and to be ritually equivalent to human blood. The traditional recipe for preparing cocoa included water and pepper, and Girolamo Benzoni, who described cocoa in his *La Historia del Mondo Nuovo*, called it a drink "more suited for pigs than for men."

Like tobacco, chocolate was initially introduced to Europe for its curative powers. Although it was used in Spain in the early 16th century, it spread to the rest of Europe only decades later. Chocolate became popular as a drink once its preparation was adapted for sweeter palates. *Traitez Nouveaux & curieux du Café, du Thé, et du Chocolate*

This Mayan terra-cotta pot (B-208 in the collection of Dumbarton Oaks, Washington, D.C.) emphasizes the religious and ritualistic aspects of cocoa in Mayan society. Cocoa pods appear to be growing out of the figure.

The first printed illustration of a cocoa tree appeared in Girolamo Benzoni's *La Historia del Mondo Nuovo*, and is reproduced here from a Venice, 1572, edition.

MONDO NVOVO. LIB. II. 103

Albero, che produce il cacauate, & come
gl'Indiani di due legni cauano fuoco.

cacauatē

IL *frutto è à modo di mandorle, & naſce in
certe zucche di groſſezza,& larghezza quaſi co
me vn cocumero, matura in termine d'vn'anno,
& eſſendo di ſtagione lo cogliono, & cacciato-
ui il frutto ſopra certe ſtuore,lo mettono al So-
le à ſciugare, & quando lo vogliono beuere, in
vn teſto lo fanno ſeccare al fuoco,& poi con
le pietre, che fanno il pane lo macinano , &
meſſolo*

THE ℬ:6:9

Indian Nectar,

OR A
DISCOURSE
CONCERNING
CHOCOLATA:
WHEREIN

The *Nature* of the *Cacao-nut*, and the other Ingredients of that Compofition, is examined, and ftated according to the Judgment and Experience of the *Indians*, and *Spanifh* Writers, who lived in the *Indies*, and others ; with fundry additional Obfervations made in *England*: The ways of *compounding* and preparing *Chocolata* are enquired into ; its Effects, as to its *alimental* and *Venereal* quality, as well as *Medicinal* (efpecially in *Hypochondriacal Melancholy*) are fully debated. Together with a *Spagyrical Analyfis* of the *Cacao-nut*, performed by that excellent Chymift, *Monfieur le Febure*, Chymift to His Majefty.

By Henry Stubbe *formerly of* Ch. Ch. *in* Oxon. *Phyfician for His Majefty, and the Right Honourable* Thomas Lord Windfor *in the Ifland of* Jamaica *in the* Weft-Indies.

Thomas Gage, Survey of the *Weft-Indies*. chap. 15.
Here [in a certain part of *Guaxaca*] *grow many Trees of* Cacao, *and* Achiote, *whereof is made the* Chocolatte, *and is a Commodity of much trading in thofe parts, though our* Englifh *and* Hollanders *make little ufe of it, when they take a prize at Sea, as not knowing the fecret virtue and quality of it for the good of the Stomach.*
——— *Videant, intabefcántque reliftâ.*

London, Printed by *J.C.* for *Andrew Crook* at the Sign of the Green Dragon in St. *Paul's* Church-yard. 1662.

In *The Indian Nectar* (London, 1662), Henry Stubbe reminded his readers of chocolate's "Indian" origins and praised its curative powers, giving special attention to its positive effects on *"hypochondriacal melancholy."*

(Lyons, 1685), by Philippe Sylvestre Dufour, became a best-seller on exotic drinks. Its third part, on chocolate, was primarily a translation of a work by the Spanish doctor Antonio Colmenero de Ledesma. It gave advice on the medicinal use of chocolate as well as recipes for enjoying it.

Chocolate, too, provoked controversy when drinking it as a panacea became the fashion in mid-17th-century Europe. Its use spread in Europe, along with an increasing demand for sugar from Caribbean plantations. To meet demands, Europeans extended the cultivation of cocoa from Mexico and Central America to the Caribbean. As chocolate's preparation became an established art, many court chefs guarded their recipes jealously, and special implements and procedures for chocolate's preparation were developed, some of them adapted from

In Dufour's *Traitez Nouveaux*, the implements for brewing chocolate depicted as belonging to "un Americain" are based on Mexican pots and swizzle sticks, although the Indian depicted is a Tupinamba from South America, where chocolate did not occur.

This plate from *De Chocolatis Potione* (Naples, 1671), by Nicephorus Sebastus Melissenus, depicts a black slave, presumably in the Caribbean, grinding and rolling chocolate paste.

The method of rolling chocolate paste seemed to change little once it was introduced into Europe. This illustration is from *Le Bon Usage du Thé, du Caffé, et du Chocolat* (Lyons, 1687), by Nicolas de Blégny.

practices followed in the New World. European recipes including such elaborate combinations as chocolate with vanilla, amber, jasmine, and cinnamon were popular with princes and prelates. Treatises like *De Chocolatis Potione* by Nicephorus Sebastus Melissenus, published in Naples in 1671 and dedicated to a cardinal, argued that chocolate could be consumed without interrupting fasting during Lent.

In England, chocolate was served in coffeehouses or in a few special establishments such as The Cocoa Tree Chocolate House or The Chocolate Room. The first advertisement for chocolate drinking, at the Queen's Head Alley in 1657, and Samuel Pepys's reference to it as his "morning draught" in 1661, suggest that new social rituals were developing around exotic delicacies. Like tobacco, chocolate had become a fashionable element of European social life but was adapted to rituals quite different from those of its place of origin.

"This Nation Is Appareled after a Thousand Fashyons"

Richard Eden, *The Decades of the Newe Worlde*, 1555

By the second half of the 16th century, information—and misinformation—about far-off and exotic parts of the world began to appear in popular books of costumes and customs. These books were attempts to describe and illustrate the dress and manners of the "whole world." People's "habits," in both senses of the word, identified them, for their costumes illustrated their customs. Intended to show how people looked and who they were, these books fed Europeans' curiosity about people who were different from themselves, especially about those from exotic lands.

Although large numbers of such books were published in numerous editions throughout Europe in the late 16th century, they contained relatively few American costumes. The same kinds of clothing and details were repeated in slightly different versions. Feathers were a major component of most illustrations of native American dress. The feather capes, headdresses, and accessories that were displayed in cabinets of curiosities probably constituted a primary source for artists and engravers, as did actual American Indians seen in Europe and a few large collections of engravings and drawings. However, many artists seem to have copied from one another, never actually having seen Americans in their native dress. Although costume books were meant to disseminate information about foreign cultures, the renderings were not always accurate and did not reflect the diversity of the dress and customs of the New World.

40 Abraham de Bruyn (1540–1587)
*Omnium Pene Europae, Asiae, Aphricae atque
Americae Gentium Habitus*

    [Antwerp], Michel Colijn, [1581]
    Shelf mark: GT 513 B8 1581 Cage

Abraham de Bruyn's influential and important book went through several editions before any American figures were included. In this 1581 version, an Indian couple in America, a noble American woman, and Athabalipa, the last American king, are shown with other "Indians" from the Orient, Africa, and the Moorish kingdom of Granada. As in most costume books, each figure stands alone without landscape or background. A social hierarchy is suggested not only by the labels differentiating the noble Americans from the

Indian couple but also by the Americans' postures, gestures, and the implements they carry.

De Bruyn appears to have used as his model a book published in Nuremberg in 1577 by Hans Weigel and Jost Amman, entitled *Habitus praecipuorum populorum*. His American couple is based on figures in the Weigel-Amman work, which were labeled as being from Brazil and Peru, or "newen Insulea," and his noble woman is based on a figure labeled as a woman in India. His source for the figure of Athabalipa is unknown.

41 Jost Amman (1539–1591)
    Gynaeceum, sive Theatrum Mulierum
        Frankfurt, Sigismund Feyerabend, 1586
        Shelf mark: GT 585 A7 Cage

At the end of the 16th century, European artists had available to them a limited stock of images of non-European peoples and their customs. Whole societies were reduced to one or two, often inaccurate, examples in costume books. This engraving of a Peruvian woman, "Foemina Peruviana," first appeared in the 1577 work of Weigel and Amman, where it was labeled "Ein Möhrin auss Granata" (A Moor of Granada) and the costume described as domestic, or indoor, wear: "Wo sie in irem Hauss umbgehn." This figure was copied by de Bruyn (cat. no. 40) as a Moor of Granada. Amman's re-use of it as a woman of Peru is indicative of the extent to which anything "Indian," "savage," "oriental," or "exotic" might be interchanged.

42   Ulisse Aldrovandi (1522–1605?)
      Ornithologiae, vol. 1
         Bologna, Giovanni Battista Bellagamba for
         Francesco dei Franceschi, 1599
         Shelf mark: QL 673 A6 1599 Cage

In descriptions of Native Americans, many early European explorers paid particular attention to the natives' "nudity"—real or fictitious, partial or total—and often used it to make moral judgments. There grew from these accounts (influenced by implements and ornaments on display in private collections) an image of "America," scantily clothed but with accessories that almost always included feathers. The private collection of the botanist and zoologist Ulisse Aldrovandi included pre-Columbian feather objects, which appear to have had a special interest for him. Here, in his massive *Ornithologiae*, are reproduced two paintings that were made for him, one of a naked Brazilian man in a feather headdress and the other of a "Queen of the Island of Florida." Details of their clothing or ornaments appear at the bottom of the engravings.

43   John Bulwer (fl. 1654)

Anthropometamorphosis: Man Transform'd

London, W. Hunt, 1653

Shelf mark: B 5461

Bulwer's book was published about 50 years after the golden age of costume books. He was more concerned with the cosmetic treatment of the body than with the ornaments and clothing that covered it. Praising the "state of nature," Bulwer criticized the "Artificiall Changling" for abusing the body by such practices as stretching ears, piercing nostrils, and changing the hairline or the shape of the nose.

The inhabitants of the New World were included in his survey of such customs. The Brazilians were said to decorate themselves by cicatrization (scar formation at the site of a healing wound—actually an African, not a Brazilian, practice), and they and the "Floridians" were correctly described as using tattoos. He also described the "feathered nations," showing naked bodies completely covered with feathers except for "the face and palmes of their hands." Although Bulwer cannot be considered a reliable source of information, he based his work on wide reading and "diligent looking not only into Civill Societies, but prying also into ruder crowds and silvestrous hordes." Works like Bulwer's had wide appeal at the time, as did the many books on "monsters."

Slash'd bodies
like cut lea-
ther Jerkins,

458   *Man Transform'd* : Or,

Cœlestiall colour from top to toe, and as an augmentation of beauty cut, gash and pinck their naked skins, which in the Relators (contrarying their) opinion, rather breeds horrour than affectation in any Traveller.

Lindscot. lib.1. cap.22.   The people of *Cambaia* and *Sian*, that dwell upon the hils called *Gueos*, marke all their bodies with hot irons, which they esteeme a freedome.

Lindscot, lib 2.   The *Brasileans*, such as would be accounted manly and stout, cut great slashes in their breasts, armes, and thighs, whereby they make the flesh to rise, which they cover with a certain powder, and make them looke blacke; which

colour never goeth off during their lives, whereby, a far off, they seeme to have cut leather Jerkins on their bodies, such as the *Switzers* use to weare.

I very easily see how many of these relations will seeme horrible untruths, but let them thinke that such narrations which consist with the reason of depraved nature, are not too sceptically to be entertained; for, because

The Artificiall Changling.   459   Bodies painted with faire branches,

because you have seen no such thing done to withdraw your beliefe, is a signe of singular pride and impudence: and he who concludes that these actions were done or not done in these places, according to his own froward opinion and assent, is halfe mad, and fit to begin a voyage to Anticyra. I confesse, writing of things that seeme so strange, a man had need walke with his Guides, which you see I have orderly done. I have brought many witnesses that give evidence point-blanck to my purpose; I alleadge Authorities, and have said nothing but what stands with some reason, and is made good by the Relators, the burthen of the lyes, if there be any, must rest upon other mens shoulders, and not on mine.

The *Brasileans* and *Florideans*, for the most part, are painted over the body, the armes, and thighs, with faire branches, whose painting can never be taken away, because they are pricked within the flesh, notwithstanding many Brasileans do paint only their bodies, (without incision) when they list; and

The Auther of the description of Nova Francia, lib.2. Lindscot, lib 2.

O o o 3   this

"The Wonders of the World Abroad"

—Shakespeare, *Two Gentlemen of Verona*

The curiosity and sense of wonder generated by the unusual plant and animal specimens, clothing, and artifacts from the New World led some prosperous collectors to want to acquire exotic objects for themselves. The resulting cabinets of curiosities, or wonder cabinets, were collections of marvelous and strange objects, both natural and manmade, from around the world. These precursors of our modern

The cabinet of the Italian naturalist Ferrante Imperato (1550–1625), as illustrated in his *Dell'historia naturale* (Naples, 1599). Reproduced with the permission of Houghton Library, Harvard University.

museums, which had come into being by the mid-16th century, comprised both princely collections, such as that of the Medici family, and those formed by learned men like the naturalist Ulisse Aldrovandi.

As the words curiosity and wonder imply, these cabinets were initially intended to entertain their viewers. The materials were not organized and classified as they would be in modern museums but were arranged according to schemes determined by their owners, sometimes distinguishing what was "natural" from what was "artificial." The great princely cabinets housing large quantities of rarities or exotica brought fame to their owners. The collections of men of learning were used for study, but they too emphasized exotic items from newly explored areas of the world. Both types of collectors publicized their cabinets, often through printed catalogues. Visitors from all over Europe and from a variety of social backgrounds were welcomed to many of these early museums. By the end of the 17th century, however, the sense of wonder had begun to wane. Collectors became more specialized, and cabinets developed into centers for instruction and study rather than entertainment.

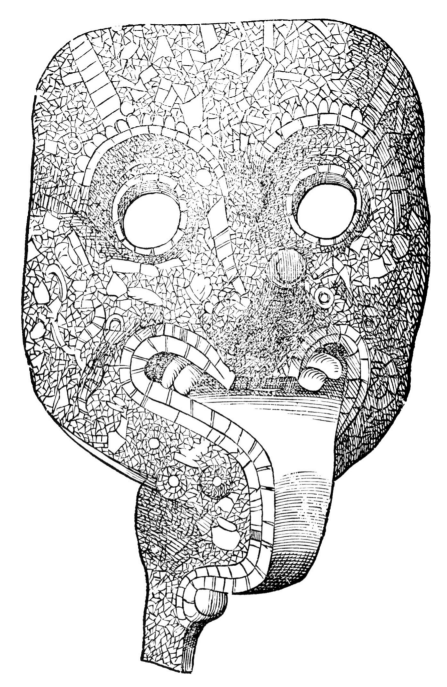

44   Ulisse Aldrovandi (1522–1605?)
      Musaeum Metallicum . . . Bartholomaeus
      Ambrosinus . . . composuit
         Bologna, Giovanni Battista Ferroni, 1648
         Shelf mark: ac 168663

Since Aldrovandi was a professor of natural history
at the University of Bologna, it is not surprising
that his famous collection emphasized the natural
sciences and contained many shells and embalmed
and stuffed mammals and fish. Aldrovandi was

intensely interested in the New World and talked
of organizing an expedition to Mexico to explore
the country's flora and fauna. Although the expedition never took place, Aldrovandi did collect
numerous artifacts and specimens from America,
including this Aztec mosaic mask, which is now in
the Museo Preistorico Etnografico in Rome. Aldrovandi gave his collection to the Senate of Bologna
in 1603. This catalogue of part of the collection
was published 43 years after Aldrovandi's death.

45   Lorenzo Legati (d. 1675)
Museo Cospiano
Bologna, Giacomo Monti, 1677
Shelf mark: ac 182448

Another Bolognese collection was that of the nobleman Ferdinando Cospi (1619–1686), a relative of the Medici family. He assembled his collection as a young man, without any particular regard for the scientific or historical importance of the items. In 1657 Cospi transferred his collection to the Palazzo Pubblico where it could be seen along with Aldrovandi's. He chose Lorenzo Legati, another naturalist who had studied many of the objects in the Aldrovandi collection, to catalogue his museum, including these two mosaic knife handles from Mexico. They, like part of Aldrovandi's collection (cat. no. 44), are now in the Museo Preistorico Etnografico in Rome.

46   Vincenzo Cartari (b. c. 1500)
Imagini delli dei de gl'antichi
Venice, Nicolo Pezzana, 1674
Shelf mark: BL 720 C2 1674 Cage

Cartari's book on the gods of the ancients was frequently reissued, in several languages, in the second half of the 16th and throughout the 17th century. An appendix entitled "Imagini degli dei indiani," by Lorenzo Pignoria (1571–1631), was added to the book in 1615 and appeared with subsequent editions. Pignoria's "Indian gods" encompassed the deities of China, Japan, and Mexico. Among the images of Mexican gods are two based on figures in the cabinet of the duke of Bavaria, one of which is reproduced here. Pignoria claimed to have received drawings of them from a scholar who held a position at the Bavarian court. The seated figure depicts a *zemi*, or idol, from the West Indies, which had been described in a 1598 inventory of the Munich cabinet. It has not survived, but the illustration resembles a *zemi* from Santo Domingo, preserved in Turin.

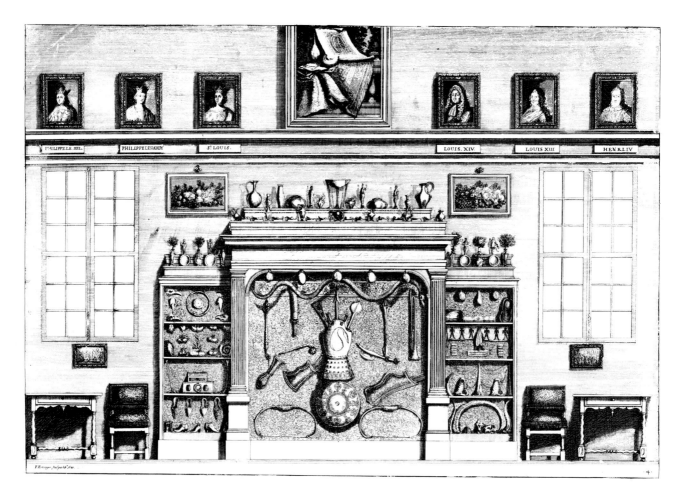

47   Claude du Molinet (1620–1687)
      Le Cabinet de la Bibliotheque de Sainte-Genevieve
         Paris, Antoine Dezallier, 1692
         Shelf mark: AM 101 D9 1692 Cage

In 1675 a new library was built for the abbey of Sainte-Geneviève in Paris. Its keeper, Claude du Molinet, stated that the library would be enhanced by "a cabinet of rare and curious pieces which would have a bearing on learning and serve the literary arts." Among the items illustrated in the catalogue of the cabinet, which du Molinet compiled, were a number of artifacts from the New World. They were not described in any detail but were referred to by du Molinet in the preface as "kinds of habits and arms of foreign countries, of the Persians, Indians, and Americans." They are illustrated in this engraving, signed by the artist F. Ertinger in 1688, as they must have appeared at that time. Displayed as trophies and curiosities, which did not require any scientific comment, these objects were spared the fate of many other collections and were not dispersed during the French Revolution. Most of the American objects in the engraving are still in the Bibliothèque Sainte-Geneviève (see cat. nos. 48–53).

48   Ball-headed club
        From northeastern North America
        Late 16th or early 17th century
        Wood and shell beads, l. 51 cm
        Bibliothèque Sainte-Geneviève, Paris
        Réserve inv. 1943, no. 128

This club, probably made by the Indians of southern New England or the Iroquois of New York, is
of hardwood, possibly maple, which has been
incised and inlaid on its back with shell beads,
known as wampum. Acquired for the Sainte-
Geneviève cabinet before 1687 (see cat. no. 47),
it apparently had been in the collection of Nicolas Claude Fabri de Peiresc (1580–1637), who
gathered many objects through regular correspondence with missionaries. It may then have
been owned by Achille de Harlay (1629–1712).
Many objects in the cabinet of the Bibliothèque
Sainte-Geneviève passed through these two
collections.

    A similar club is held by the Indian standing
at Captain Smith's head in the lower right-hand
corner of the engraving from Smith's *Generall Historie of Virginia* (cat. no. 22).

49 Ceremonial baton

> From northeastern South America
> Early 17th century?
> Wood, paint, resin, and fiber, l. 68 cm
> Bibliothèque Sainte-Geneviève, Paris
> Réserve inv. 1943, no. 145

Made of hardwood partially painted and covered
with vegetable fibers and resin, this ceremonial
baton is probably from Arawak or Carib Indians of
the Guiana region. The kneeling figure at the top
of the baton rests his hands on two severed heads,
presumably trophies of a battle. The base of the
baton bears painted decoration resembling that on
archaeological pottery from the mouth of the
Amazon. It was acquired sometime before 1687
(see cat. no. 47) and had probably been in the collections of Nicolas Claude Fabri de Peiresc (1580–
1637) and Achille de Harlay (1629–1712).

50   Club *(detail)*

From northeastern South America
17th century
Wood and putty or paint, l. 142 cm
Bibliothèque Sainte-Geneviève, Paris
Réserve inv. 1943, no. 144

Made of a hardwood, the club has been incised and
then filled in with putty or paint. The geometric
decoration probably has symbolic significance. It is
typical of clubs from the Brazil/Guiana border
region, many of which entered early European collections. This is one of two in the Sainte-Geneviève
cabinet that were acquired sometime before 1687.
Almost certainly this is the one illustrated in du
Molinet (cat. no. 47).

51   Anchor axe

From Brazil or Guiana
16th or 17th century
Stone, wood, cord, and feathers, l. 49 cm
Bibliothèque Sainte-Geneviève, Paris
Réserve inv. 1943, no. 130

Axes of this type, called anchor axes because of
the shape of the blade, are thought to be from the
Gê-speaking tribes of eastern Brazil. The cord
wrapped around and glued to the wooden handle
preserves traces of red feathers that had been glued
to the handle. The axe was acquired for the Sainte-
Geneviève cabinet before 1687 (see cat. no. 47).
There were probably others in European cabinets, for an anchor axe is sometimes among the
attributes of early allegorical figures representing
America. In the border of the world map from
Linschoten's *Navigatio ac Itinerarium* (1599; cat. no.
82), a female figure representing Peru holds a long-
handled axe with a similar blade.

52   Club

From Brazil
17th century
Wood, l. 132 cm
Bibliothèque Sainte-Geneviève, Paris
Réserve inv. 1943, no. 146

This club, of a type known only from the
Tupinamba Indians of coastal Brazil, appears complete in the 1692 engraving in du Molinet's catalogue (see cat. no. 47). However, part of the
rounded head and the blade of the club have been
lost since the end of the 17th century. Undoubtedly intended for use in the ritual killing of prisoners of war, clubs of this type appear frequently
in 16th- and 17th-century European representations of American Indians. Numerous examples
must have made their way into European cabinets,
and more than ten have recently been identified in
old European collections. This one was acquired by
the Bibliothèque Sainte-Geneviève prior to 1687.
The butt has been reworked, perhaps when it was
installed in the exhibit shown in the engraving.

A club of this type is propped against a tree in
the engraving entitled *America* from Jan van der
Straet's *Nova reperta* (cat. no. 3). Another example
is found on the title page to Abraham Ortelius's
Theatrum Orbis Terrarum (1595) held by the female
figure of America (cat. no. 81). Thevet illustrated
such a club in use (see p. 115, Vaughan, "Salvages
and Men of Ind," below).

53 Collar (?)

From South America
17th century
Bark and fiber, external diam. 32 cm
Bibliothèque Sainte-Geneviève, Paris
Réserve inv. 1943, no. 157

The provenance of this object, which is presumably a neck ring or collar, is uncertain. It is probably from central Brazil, because clubs among Indians of the Xingú-Tocantins area have shafts wrapped with plaited basketry similar to that on this ring. No object resembling this form, however, has yet been documented from South America. Six decorative rings on the collar are made of braided bark. This object was added to the Sainte-Geneviève collection before 1687 (see cat. no. 47).

The New World on Display

European Pageantry and the Ritual Incorporation of the Americas

Steven Mullaney

The world Columbus "discovered" in 1492 was a rather well-populated one. Demographic historians estimate that the total pre-Columbian population of the Western hemisphere fell somewhere between 57 and 112 million people—that is, a population either approximately equal to, or considerably larger than, the total population of Europe itself during the same period. Over the next century, however, New World cultures suffered a general rate of decline of approximately two-thirds, and for many the death rate was even more precipitous. For example, the island of Española (commonly anglicized as Hispaniola) may have been home to as many as 8 million people before European contact. By 1518, however, the native Taino population was under 100,000 and still declining rapidly; long before 1600, the Taino had disappeared entirely. Those peoples and individuals who survived both the ecological catastrophe of unfamiliar diseases—by far the greatest cause of death on such a staggering scale—and the violence of armed conquest suffered long-term processes of colonization that transformed their cultures, or what little remained of them, radically and forever after.[1]

Human and cultural devastation on such a scale is difficult to take in fully or adequately; at the least, such statistics serve as a necessary reminder that, for the aboriginal inhabitants of the Americas, Columbus's voyage of 1492 had consequences as stark as they are undeniable. When we turn to the question of the impact of the New World on the Old, however, Europe sometimes seems remarkably untouched by what we imagine should have been, for it, a cultural encounter of great significance. From the perspective of Europe, after all, the Americas *were* a new world: Europeans had no prior knowledge of the diverse lands and cultures they encountered there. Yet despite the great many books devoted to the Americas in the 16th century, the Old World was generally incurious and uninquisitive about the New, even as it explored and conquered it and stripped it of its riches. As J. H. Elliott has noted, 16th-century cosmographers continued to describe the world as if the Western hemisphere were unknown; political and social philosophers made scant if any use of information about New World societies and peoples. "One of the most striking features of sixteenth-century intellectual history," Elliott concludes, "[was] the apparent slowness of Europe in making the mental adjustments required to incorporate America within its field of vision."[2]

Printed travel accounts and learned works were not the only means by which Europeans were exposed to aspects of the New World, of course. In European ritual and pageantry, ranging from civic processions and wedding festivals to royal entries (see cat. nos. 54–60), America was brought into Europe's "field of vision" in a quite literal sense, as an ensemble of images, customs, and peoples to be displayed, represented, and performed before audiences of all walks of life and, in some instances, of every class. Since these elaborately staged public spectacles and displays were accessible to the literate and illiterate alike, far more people were likely to have taken notice, at least, of some aspect of the New World by such means, and there was

The duc de Guise as the American king from Charles Perrault, *Festiva ad Capita Annulumque Decursio, a Rege Ludovico XIV* (Paris, 1670).

ample opportunity to do so. Although no one has attempted a systematic or complete survey, Indians in feather skirts and headdresses—an early and well-established mode of representing any New World native—appear with regular frequency in ballets, wedding celebrations, and official processions ranging from Lord Mayor's pageants to royal entries.[3] Although such "Indian" figures are often marginal, they sometimes occupy center stage, as in the elaborate carousel held by Louis XIV in 1662, during which the duc de Guise appeared as a fantastically attired American Indian king (see cat. no. 57). Even when more ethnographically accurate, however, most festive depictions of New World figures and themes remain entirely superficial, with little if any relation to reality. Here, too, Europe's capacity and desire to apprehend the New World, to address either the general significance of the Americas or the particular and unique characteristics of the peoples encountered there, are less than impressive. Indians from the Americas are often confused with Eastern or Asian figures; even when depicted with fair accuracy (at least according to established iconographic tradition), they are mistaken for Moors.[4] Not even learned observers could always

decipher the feathers and parrots that were the representational markers of New World natives. Commenting on characters thus accoutered in *La finta pazza*, a play staged in Paris in 1645, Lefebvre d'Ormesson calls them a group of "Ethiopians and parrots."[5] It would seem that exotic and alien races, whether new or old, were difficult for 16th-century Europeans to tell apart.

When Indian figures were not confused with other alien races or cultures, their strangeness could provoke an analogical reflection on strange figures closer to home—an alienating reflection on the increasingly important, because increasingly troublesome, ethnic subcultures of the Old World. "We have Indians at home," as one Englishman observed, "Indians in Cornwall, Indians in Wales, Indians in Ireland."[6] In the case of Ireland especially, given the dark history of 16th-century English colonial practices in that land, such an analogy could hardly be described as salutary. And when Indians were merely mistaken for other races, as in the examples above, the reason for such confusion appears to lie in the generic role that New World themes, artifacts, and figures played in festivities and processions. They were first and foremost a register of the strange, the exotic, or the alien, only secondarily a register of a new world, and they were incorporated into existing structures of festivity as but one of a number of more familiar examples. That is to say, their inclusion altered neither the structure of whatever ritual or celebration they were a part of, nor the structures of perception of those who witnessed them. A clear but particularly elaborate instance is provided by the month-long festivities celebrating the wedding of Cosimo de' Medici II and Maria Magdalena in 1608. On the eleventh day of the wedding celebrations, the townspeople of Florence were treated to a mock battle staged on the Santa Trinità bridge, during which a group of Pisan noblemen fought and defeated warriors from "every foreign land."[7] The description was apparently not as hyperbolic as it might seem. Along the lower border of the illustration of

The mock battle staged on the Santa Trinità bridge from Camillo
Rinuccini, *Descrizione Delle Feste Fatte Nelle Reali Nozze* (Florence, 1608).

Il Giuoco del ponte, as the entertainment was
known, are 18 examples, ancient and modern,
ranging from Roman centurions to contemporary
Moors, Greeks, and Germans (and even such
mythical figures as a Cyclops, a Merman, and a
Lion-man). Their individual and distinctive costumes are depicted in great detail, in part to
convey the considerable expense taken to equip
many if not all the armies of the known world,
and all for a single day's celebration. Prominent
on the banks of the river, where the foreign soldiers are in procession, is a group of American
Indians with the requisite feather skirts, headdresses, and spears (see cat. no. 58). Like the
other exotic warriors, they too did battle with
the Pisan nobles, and like the others they suffered defeat.

The inclusion of feathered warriors from the
New World was clearly superficial; without it,
the display of Pisan valor and prowess would
have been the same, the ranks of foreign oppo-
nents merely reduced by one. But the superficial
is not the same as the insignificant. In such an
assimilation of the New World into the Old, a
festive diminution of the exotic or strange is
accomplished by means of its inclusion. The genuinely novel is incorporated into a preexisting
structure that to a large extent obscures novelty,
and in this sense the ritual or festive incorpora-

tion of America duplicates certain facets of the
intellectual attitude of the Old World to the
New, especially its tendency to process the new
by lodging it within traditional and established
patterns of thought.

In other instances, however, the ceremonial
portrayal of the New World exhibits greater
complexity, even showing signs of some ambivalence toward European colonization. Such is the
case with one of the New World decorations
created for the 1634 entry into Antwerp of
Prince Ferdinand, brother of Philip IV and
the new Spanish governor of the Netherlands
(see cat. no. 56). As Ferdinand made his way
through the city he passed through a series of
arches especially constructed for his procession.
Among them was the Arch of the Mint, erected
by the Royal Mint and designed by Rubens and
Johann Gaspard Gevaerts. Seeking a theme that
would compliment both the mint and the Spanish governor, the artists designed an arch in the
form of Mount Potosí in Peru, then the richest
silver mine in the world and the pride of Spain's
colonial empire. Although an arch in the form of
a mountain was an unusual approach for processional architecture, it was not altogether unprecedented, and the Rubens-Gevaerts design may
have been influenced both by one of the arches
erected for Henri II's triumphal entry into Rouen

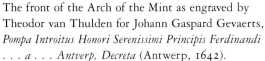

The front of the Arch of the Mint as engraved by Theodor van Thulden for Johann Gaspard Gevaerts, *Pompa Introitus Honori Serenissimi Principis Ferdinandi . . . a . . . Antverp, Decreta* (Antwerp, 1642).

The rear of the Arch of the Mint as engraved by van Thulden.

in 1550 and by the engraved title page of Theodor de Bry's *Americae pars sexta*.[8] What is at once distinct and peculiar about the Arch of the Mint, however, is the contrast between the scenes depicted on its front and rear faces.

On the front of the arch, the columns of the portal merge into the rough and massive boulders of Potosí, creating an unusual combination of sculptured and unworked, craggy stone relief. On top of the mountain is a tree framed by two figures: on the right is Jason, who is about to pluck the golden fleece from the tree, and on the left is the figure of Felicitas, who both represents and guarantees a happy voyage. Lower down on the left side of the façade are figures representing the region of gold; on the right is the realm of silver, and each side is governed

respectively by the sun and the moon, which rest upon the twin pillars of Hercules (the emblem of Charles V, during whose reign the Spanish conquest was begun). A profile of Philip IV appears on a medallion just under the tree at the top, and the inscription grants him the title of *locupletator orbis terrarum*, the benefactor of the world.

Despite the various symbols and emblems of the *conquistadores* (whom Gevaerts styled "the new Jasons and Argonauts")[9] and the epic presence of Jason himself, the front of the arch conveys a sense of stately accomplishment that is neither martial nor violent, and the depiction of Jason, notwithstanding the unavoidable epic connotations, is almost pastoral in its sense of calmness and ease. Parrots perch on the tree, and although a guardian dragon lies at its foot, the serpent is either sleeping or already vanquished. Although Jason wears classical armor, his sword is sheathed, and the fleece hangs from the tree like a ripe fruit waiting to be plucked. The rear of the arch, however, conveys a different mood entirely. Realistic depiction of arduous, forced labor replaces stately allegory: on the left, two workmen wield pickaxes against the rock, while on the right, two laborers—one of them beardless and with a cap of tightly curled hair, his features more African than Peruvian—emerge from the mouth of a mine, nearly doubled over from the heavy loads of ore on their backs. At the top of the mountain is another tree, but the scene under it is a violent one, representing Hercules in the Garden of the Hesperides. The guardian dragon here is clearly awake and alive but is contorted in its death throes; its clawed foot is upraised and reaching out to strike, but it is about to receive another blow from the club that Hercules holds high above his head in a two-handed grip, his body coiled to deliver its full power in the next and presumably final swing. Opposite Hercules is the figure of Hispania, plucking golden apples from the tree and dropping them into a fold in her robes. The effect is one of haste and stealth, of a theft in the midst of a battle whose outcome, though presumably certain, is not yet decided.

Although it is impossible to imagine that either Rubens or Gevaerts *intended* the rear of the arch as a critical commentary on Spanish exploitation of New World inhabitants and resources— artists were not paid commissions to insult their aristocratic audiences—it is equally impossible, from my own perspective, to view the two scenes without a sense of extreme contradiction. What is easy and decorous, almost an act of Nature rather than an exploit of Man, on the front of the arch is brutal and violent on the rear; it is almost as if we were given two incompatible views of Spanish wealth and its New World origins, the official myth and the harsh, underlying reality that the myth was created to obscure. The incongruity between the two views is heightened rather than

diminished when we try to imagine the arch as Ferdinand experienced it—as a three-dimensional portal through which he passed, erected at the entrance to Sint-Michielsstraat. Theodor van Thulden portrayed the front and the rear of the arch in separate engravings, and this is how Ferdinand would have viewed the two scenes—first the front side, then the rear, never having both in view at once, except of course where front and rear can no longer be defined—that is, at the top of Mount Potosí, where both Jason and Hercules, Felicitas and Hispania, enact their contrasting scenes under a tree. Was there one tree, or two? Although we know very little about the actual construction of the Arch of the Mint, we know that it was indeed built, the two-dimensional, separate etchings translated into a single three-dimensional form, and we can safely assume that, no matter how skilled, the craftsmen of Antwerp could not violate the laws of nature to allow two pairs of figures and two contrasting scenes to occupy the same physical space. Presumably the top of Mount Potosí was broad enough to encompass two trees and two contrasting pairs of figures. But even so, the known dimensions of the arch were not sufficiently large to eliminate—as van Thulden's etchings do—the shadowy glimpse of one scene behind the other, of the violence, theft, labor, and death that lay behind and adumbrated the wealth of these "new Jasons and Argonauts." Although successfully built, the Arch of the Mint was still, in a sense, an impossible construct, folding two incongruent versions of Spanish wealth and Mount Potosí into one architectural figure—an immense and concrete realization of a contradiction that lay at the heart of colonial ideology.[10]

As I suggested earlier, the inclusion of New World figures and customs in European pageantry was often superficial and, when not entirely fanciful, still bore little relation to American realities. Such inattention to ethnographic detail was not always the case, however, as a final example from France will illustrate.[11] In 1550, a meadow bordering on the Seine and located on the outskirts of Rouen was planted with trees and shrubs, some natural, some artificial, all foreign to the locale and all combining to create the semblance of a Brazilian forest landscape (see cat. no. 54). The trees were painted red, the color of the brazilwood that was the basis of the city's New World lumber trade. From the reports of those present, it was a re-creation convincing to the knowing and well-traveled observer, both in what it revealed and in what it left concealed. The foliage was at certain points impenetrable to the eye, allowing the simulated forest to serve as habitat and refuge for the parrots, marmots, and apes that had been set at large within it. The *bons bourgeois* of the city had also constructed two authentically detailed Brazilian villages, the huts carved from solid tree trunks at great labor but "in true native fashion." The villages themselves were stocked with over 50 "Tabbagerres" and "Toupinaboux" (Tupinamba) Indians freshly imported for the occasion. Supplementing the genuine Brazilians were some 250 Frenchmen appropriately costumed—"sans aucunement couvrir la partie que nature commande" —and drawn from the ranks of seamen, merchants, and adventurers who had been to Brazil and knew the manners, customs, and tongues of the tribes involved. "It all seemed real," as an account published in 1551 testified, "and not at all simulated."[12]

The occasion was Henri II's royal entry into Rouen: an event that can hardly explain the genesis of one of the most thorough performances of a New World culture staged by the Renaissance, but does at least illuminate the pragmatic function of Brazil in the ongoing dramaturgy of city and state. A delicate negotiation of power and prestige was at once necessitated and accomplished by a monarch's passage into an early modern city of any size. In keeping with the conventions of the Roman Triumph as it was transformed and elaborated by the Renaissance, it had become customary for a monarch and his entourage to pause outside the city gates, on the threshold of the community, at that tenuous point where royal domain shaded into civic jurisdiction. Halting there made the royal visitor more a spectator than an actor in the drama at hand, and prompted by his gaze, a mock battle or sciamachy (a custom we also observed, in different

form, in the Medici wedding in Florence) would commence. Oftentimes the martial triumphs thus staged would celebrate the royal spectator's own military prowess and accomplishments. A mock siege was common. A castle erected on the margins of the city would be stormed and taken: rather than lay siege to gain entry, the monarch granted an entry was entertained by the comfortably displaced spectacle of a siege, a dramatic enactment that at once represented the potential for conflict manifested by a royal visit and sublimated that potential, recasting it as a cultural performance to be enjoyed by city and crown alike. When Queen Isabella of Bavaria entered Paris in 1389, it was only after watching Saladin and his Saracens defend a castle that was eventually taken by Richard Coeur de Lion; at Rome in 1492, in commemoration of the victory at Granada, Spanish troops stormed a wooden castle occupied by citizens in Moors' clothing.[13]

Henri did not witness a siege, but he did view what the imperial ambassador described as "a sham combat illustrating the manner of fighting in Brazil."[14] Before the battle began, however, the royal party lingered for some time, delighted with the convincing performance of natives real and counterfeit as they went about their daily rounds. Such a delay marked a temporary suspension in the momentum of the king's entry—lingering on the threshold not only of the city but also of the sciamachy which customarily manifested that threshold—but the breach in ceremonial decorum was understandable. The *Figure des Brisilians* that accompanies the official account of the entry shows men hunting monkeys with arrows and spears and scaling trees to gather the fruit that was either lashed in place or growing there. A group of men and women dance in a clearing, their hands joined in a circle reminiscent of European May-games. Couples stroll arm in arm through the foliage; toward the right-hand margin of the scene, a man and a woman strike a pose that recalls period illustrations of Genesis. Yet the tableau is polymorphous, overdetermined in the sense that it represents more than a single scene should be able to contain. Along with its version of Edenic pastoral

The Brazilian forest landscape created in Rouen, from *C'est la Deduction du sumptueux ordre plaisantz spectacles* (Rouen, 1551).

it reveals a land of unbiblical license and enterprise. Some of the couples are partially obscured in the underbrush, taking advantage of the cover to indulge in relatively unabashed foreplay; men are hewing trees, then carrying them to the river to build primitive barks. The soft primitivism of biblical tradition coexists with a harder interpretation of pagan cultures, akin to the portraits of barbaric life composed by Piero di Cosimo.[15]

What we have is a detailed mise-en-scène of Brazilian culture, re-creating even the moment of the natives' capture—on the Seine, a French merchant ship is under sail, gradually approaching the bank where a group of naked and unknowing figures awaits its arrival[16]—and the projection of European libido and myth onto that scene. The New World is both re-created in the suburbs of the Old and made over into an alternate version of itself, strange but capable of imagination. Dominating the field of the spectacle, a man and woman occupy a hammock stretched between two trees. The two are naked like those below them, but even so they are invested with a regal bearing; the man holds a scepter, and both figures wear crowns that contrast sharply with the leaves and fronds worn as headgear by their savage subjects. Simi-

larly crowned but fully cloaked in the robes of state, watching his heathen surrogate from the vantage point of a scaffold placed at the edge of the meadow, Henri must have been especially pleased to find a version of himself and his queen, Catherine de Médicis, thus occupying the scene he beheld. A major theme of the day would be revealed in the final emblematic display of the entry, in the heart of the city, where Henri's father would be praised "for having restored letters and saved [Rouen] from barbarism,"[17] and Henri himself would be admonished to follow in his father's footsteps. It was a duty foreshadowed, its barbaric metaphor cast into more literal terms in these figures of primitive patriarchy, raised above the savage scene they commanded, over which they ruled.

At some point, fighting broke out between the two tribes: the mock battle or sciamachy which was the pretense of this elaborate scene had commenced. One tribe decimated the ranks of the other, then burned its village to the ground. In most royal entries, the carefully and expensively created tableau would have served its purpose at this point and be dismantled once the sovereign had passed beyond it into the city. But Rouen's designs for Brazil were not yet consummated because Brazil, or this European version of it, was not yet fully consumed. On the following day victor and vanquished would trade roles, for the entire triumph was repeated in an encore performance for Catherine's own entry, during which the second village, faithfully and elaborately fashioned so as to be "le certain simulacre de la verité," was also set ablaze and reduced to ash. The re-creation of Brazil had been surprisingly detailed and complete, and its consummation followed suit. It was the age of conspicuous expenditure and ostentatious display; what was displayed in public ceremony was often, in one sense or another, used up in the process, consummation being in fact the point: what you had was most clearly manifested by how much you could afford to expend in lavish and costly celebration.[18] But the consumption of Brazil can hardly be explained by such generalities of early modern culture. What was most conspicuously expended in this instance was neither money, time, nor other indigenous resources, but an alien culture itself, at least in terms of theatrical representation. It is difficult to say which is more awesome: the painstaking expense of spirit and wealth that went into such a carefully reconstructed and authenticated verisimilitude or the thoroughness with which it was all effaced, even though full effacement required a full-scale repetition of the entire entry.

Representation is always a form of repetition, but in the two-day course of events at Rouen both representation and re-presentation, imitation and repeated performance, conspired to achieve a paradoxical end—not the affirmation of what was thus represented and repeated, but its erasure or negation. Earlier I suggested that entirely superficial treatments of the New World in European pageantry reveal a significant pattern in Renaissance Europe's approach to the new and the strange, that including strange things and peoples in traditional structures of ritual and thought served not to clarify what was unique about them or to foster genuine understanding but to diminish their strangeness and to a degree to efface what was thus included. Although hardly superficial in its treatment of the New World, Henri's entry into Rouen clarifies this pattern and takes it to its fullest extreme. The ethnographic attention and knowledge displayed at Rouen was genuine, amazingly thorough, and richly detailed; the object, however, was not to understand Brazilian culture but to perform it, in a paradoxically self-consuming fashion. Knowledge of another culture in such an instance is directed toward ritualistic rather than ethnological ends, and the rite involved is one ultimately organized around the elimination of its own pretext: the spectacle of the other that is thus celebrated and observed, in passing. To speak of Renaissance curiosity or fascination with other cultures barely begins to address what is odd in such an anthropology, geared not toward the interpretation of strange cultures but toward their consummate performance.[19] What is thus performed, the simulacrum of Brazilian culture, is fully eliminated in this ritual processing of the new and the strange—although as far as we know, the demise of the Brazilians themselves was simulated and not real, at least when staged in the Old World rather than the New.

Steven Mullaney is Associate Professor of English, University of Michigan, Ann Arbor

Notes

1. For the population of Española in 1492, see Sherburne F. Cook and Woodrow Borah, *Essays in Population History* (Berkeley: University of California Press, 1971), vol. 1. For low and high estimates of hemispheric population, see respectively William M. Denevan, ed., *The Native Population of the Americas in 1492* (Madison: University of Wisconsin Press, 1976), pp. 290–291, and Henry F. Dobyns, "Estimating Aboriginal American Population: An Appraisal of Techniques with a New Hemispheric Estimate," *Current Anthropology* 7 (1966): 415. In his recent study, *American Indian Holocaust and Survival: A Population History since 1492* (Norman and London: University of Oklahoma Press, 1987), Russell Thornton arrives at a minimum figure of 72 million.

2. J. H. Elliott, *The Old World and the New, 1492–1650* (London: Cambridge University Press, 1970), p. 8.

3. For a selective survey and discussion of some examples, see Suzanne Boorsch, "America in Festival

Presentations," in *First Images of America*, ed. Fredi Chiapelli (Berkeley: University of California Press, 1976), vol. 1, pp. 503–515.

4. This is the case in a German fête inaugurating Leopold I as Holy Roman Emperor in 1658; see Boorsch, "America," p. 505.

5. Quoted in Boorsch, "America," p. 505.

6. Quoted in Christopher Hill, *Change and Continuity in Seventeenth-Century England* (London: Weidenfeld and Nicolson, 1974), p. 20.

7. Camillo Rinuccini, *Descrizione Delle Feste Fatte Nelle Reali Nozze De' Serenissimi Principi Di Toscana D. Cosimo De' Medici, E Maria Maddalena Arciduchessa D'Austria in Firenze* (Florence, 1608), p. 54.

8. For this interpretation and an extended description of the arch, see John Rupert Martin, *The Decorations for the Pompa Introitus Ferdinandi* (London and New York: Phaidon, 1972), pp. 189–202.

9. Martin, *Decorations*, p. 191.

10. The task of handling the "overarching" space of a three-dimensional, freestanding processional arch—the top—was an inescapable but easily resolved problem of artistic design, at least when the artists did not choose to emphasize the architectural paradox. For an illustrative example we need look no further than the arch erected at Saint Michael's for the same entry. Here, although the scenes depicted on the front and rear faces differ, the figures at the top exactly duplicate one another, creating a visual echo rather than a critical adumbration or subversion for the viewer. For the arch at Saint Michael's, see Martin, *Decorations*, figs. 105 and 109.

11. The following account is based on and partially revises my earlier treatment of Henri II's entry into Rouen; for that version in a different but related context, see Steven Mullaney, *The Place of the Stage: License, Play, and Power in Early Modern England* (Chicago and London: University of Chicago Press, 1988), pp. 60–88.

12. Henri II's entry was chronicled in two prose accounts and one verse. The fullest, from which I have quoted, is *C'est la Deduction du sumptueux ordre plaisantz spectacles et magnifiques theatres dresses, et exhibes par les citoiens de Rouen, ville metropolitaine du pays de Normandie, à la sacree maiesté du treschristian roy de France, Henry second, leur souverain seigneur, et à tres illustre dame, ma dame Katharine de Medicis* (Rouen, 1551); reprinted as *Entrée à Rouen du Roi Henri II et de la Reine Catherine de Médicis* (Rouen, 1885). An excellent and full-length study of the entry has been made by Margaret M. McGowan,

"Form and Themes in Henri II's Entry into Rouen," *Renaissance Drama*, n.s. 1 (1968): 199–252.

In *Early Anthropology in the Sixteenth and Seventeenth Centuries* (Philadelphia: University of Pennsylvania Press, 1964), p. 112, Margaret Hodgen erroneously reports the villages outside of Bordeaux in 1565. Gilbert Chinard mentions the Bordeaux festivities parenthetically while discussing the Rouen entry, and he may be the source of confusion about the two quite different ceremonies; see Chinard, *L'exotisme Américain dans la littérature française au 16e siècle* (Paris: Hachette, 1911), pp. 105–106.

13. For the history of the use of a sciamachy in royal entries, see Sidney Anglo, "The Evolution of the Early Tudor Disguising, Pageant, and Mask," *Renaissance Drama*, n.s. 1 (1968): 13–18.

14. *Calendar of State Papers (Spanish), 1550–1552*, X:182.

15. See Erwin Panofsky, *Studies in Iconology: Humanistic Themes in the Art of the Renaissance* (New York: Harper & Row, 1962), pp. 13–18. I am indebted to Terry Comito for this reference and a clarifying discussion on the point.

16. The French ship is shown in an illuminated edition of the *Entrée*; see the reproduction in Roy Strong, *Splendor at Court: Renaissance Spectacle and the Theater of Power* (Boston: Houghton Mifflin, 1973), pp. 88–89.

17. *Calendar of State Papers (Spanish), 1550–1552*, X:182.

18. On conspicuous expenditure and its devastating effects on the English aristocracy, see Lawrence Stone, "The Anatomy of the Elizabethan Aristocracy," *The Economic History Review* 28 (1948): 3–13.

19. For efforts to "justify" Renaissance interest in other cultures as a precursor of Enlightenment ethnography, see Hodgen, *Early Anthropology*, and to a lesser degree, John Howland Rowe, "The Renaissance Foundations of Anthropology," *American Anthropologist* 67 (1965): 1–14. For an illuminating counterargument, see James A. Boon, "Comparative De-enlightenment: Paradox and Limits in the History of Ethnology," *Daedalus* 109 (1980): 73–91.

"Salvages and Men of Ind"

English Theatrical Representations
of American Indians, 1590–1690

Virginia Mason Vaughan

When Trinculo first encounters Caliban in Shakespeare's *Tempest*, he wonders whether the "monster" is a man or a fish, then speculates that, if secured and transported to London, such a creature would make a man's fortune: "any strange beast there makes a man. When they will not give a doit to relieve a lame beggar, they will lay out ten to see a dead Indian" (2.2.31–33). "Salvages and men of Ind," Trinculo's pal Stephano agrees, could be profitable. Because their strangeness promoted wonder among the populace—an "emotional and intellectual response to radical difference"[1]—the public display of a kidnapped Indian was a theatrical experience, a spectacle offered in exchange for money. It is hardly surprising that by the early 17th century English actors costumed as American Indians frequently appeared in processions and pageants and, later in the century, were heroes in tragedies. They portrayed the otherness of New World natives by wearing body paint and feather headdresses, by portraying pagan sun worship and an alien language. Yet they were never intended to render an accurate representation of Indian appearance and custom. Rather, as the 17th century progressed, Indians on stage increasingly stood for political and ideological positions. If, in the world at large, Indians were "gradually reduced to the role of 'extras' in the great drama of European expansion," as Hugh Honour observes,[2] on the English stage their conversion or conquest proclaimed England's destiny as a world power.

Although Shakespeare never directly presented a New World native to his audience (except perhaps Caliban, the son of an Algerian witch, whose Indian-ness may be suggested by his role as a dispossessed native and by references to the Bermoothes and a brave new world),[3] he did refer to Indians several times in his plays. When Helena describes her unrequited love for Bertram in *All's Well That Ends Well*, for example, she mentions the common Elizabethan notion that Indians were heathens who worshiped the sun:

> Thus Indian-like,
> Religious in mine error, I adore
> The sun, that looks upon his worshipper,
> But knows of him no more.   (1.3.204–207)

The Indians' supposed ignorance of European values is also apparent in the first quarto of *Othello*, when the Moor claims that, like the base Indian, he threw "a pearl away / Richer than all his tribe" (5.2.347). Titania, Queen of the Fairies in *A Midsummer Night's Dream*, keeps in her train a young Indian boy, "stolen from an Indian king," though this may mean the East Indies, not the West. And in one of his last dramatic efforts, Shakespeare connects the New World native with popular spectacle and bawdry; in the final scene of *Henry VIII*, the Porter urges his helper to keep out the multitude who throng to court for Princess Elizabeth's coronation. He rambles: "Or have we some strange Indian with the great tool come to court, the women so besiege us? Bless me, what a fry of fornication is at door" (5.3.34–36). Like Helena, the Porter conveys at least one conventional European view of American Indians—they were objects of won-

114

der partly because their nakedness bespoke a barbaric sexuality.

Shakespeare was not the only dramatist to allude to the New World. In George Chapman's *Eastward Hoe!* Captain Seagull praises the Indians' appreciation of beauty and suggests the possibility of their amalgamation with the English:

> A whole Country of English is there, man, bred of those that were left there in [15]79. They have married with the Indians, and make 'hem bring forth as beautifull faces as any we have in England; and therefore the Indians are so in love with 'hem, that all the treasure they have, they lay at their feete.[4]

But in the next breath, Seagull suggests that the natives do not share European attitudes toward precious metals, for "all their dripping Pans and their Chamber pottes are pure Gold" (see cat. no. 69).

Captain Seagull's ambivalence was not unique to the theater. It was strikingly characteristic of European accounts of the New World published in England during the last half of the 16th century. On the one hand, explorers' narratives depicted a barbaric image of Indians, vilifying them for cannibalism, heathenism, and incivility, as in André Thevet's *New Found Worlde*, written in 1550 and translated into English in 1568, which declared that the natives of America were "wild and bruitish people, without Fayth, without Lawe, without Religion, and without any civilitie: but living like brute beasts."[5] On the other hand, many explorers reported that the Indians had admirable qualities, especially when compared to corrupt Europeans. Jean Ribaut, a French explorer whose work appeared in England in the 1560s, praised the Indians for being "of goodly stature, mighty, faire, and as well shapen and proportioned of bodye as any people in the world, very gentill, curtious and of a good nature."[6] Or, as Montaigne argued in his essay "Of the Caniballes" (1580s; published in English 1603), Brazilian Indians may have been savage but they were still more virtuous than their French contemporaries who knew Christian truth but ignored it.[7]

"Wild and bruitish" natives of America from André Thevet, *Les Singularitez de la France Antarctique* (Antwerp, 1558).

Because English exploration had little impact until the abortive Roanoke expeditions of the 1580s, it is understandable that there were no actual representations of Indians in the popular theater during the Elizabethan period. Under the Stuart government, English settlement increased—first in Virginia, then in Massachusetts, Maryland, and elsewhere. Indians were accordingly appropriated in court entertainments, especially masques, as symbols of royal power and prerogative. Not only was every Stuart masque "an assertion of the Divine Right of kings," it was also a ritual that affirmed the rightness of the English state and its destiny as a world power.[8] The masque normally moved from a pattern of disorder (the antimasque performed by professional actors) to a climactic moment, when "the fiction opened outward to include the whole court, as masquers descended from pageant car [wagon] on stage and took partners from the audience."[9] The dance represented the orderly triumph of the aristocratic community over disorderly forces that might subvert it.

This pattern appears in George Chapman's *Memorable Maske*, an entertainment performed (as *The Tempest* may have been) in celebration of Princess Elizabeth's marriage to Frederick V, Elector Palatine in 1613 (see cat. no. 61). The wedding was a triumph for the Protestant cause, and many people hoped that the alliance signaled

England's solid alignment against Spain and other Catholic powers. But *The Memorable Maske* had other political ramifications: it was organized by the Gentlemen of the Inns of Court and included investors in the Virginia Company who sought royal patronage for their venture.

Designed by Inigo Jones and performed at Whitehall, *The Memorable Maske* began with a lavish procession of antimasque figures, including "Baboons." Next came "the choice Musitions of our Kingdome,"[10] costumed

> like Virginean Priests, by whom the Sun is there ador'd; and therfore called the Phoebades. Their Robes were tuckt up before; strange Hoods of feathers, and scallops about their neckes, and on their heads turbants, stucke with severall colour'd feathers, spotted with wings of Flies, of extraordinary bignesse; like those of their countrie: . . . Then rode the chiefe Maskers, in Indian habits, all of a resemblance; . . . under their breasts, they woare bawdricks of golde, embroidered high with purle, and about their neckes, Ruffes of feathers, spangled with pearle and silver. On their heads high sprig'd-feathers, compast in Coronets, like the Virginian Princes they presented.   (A1ᵛ–A2ʳ)

The "Indians'" ruffs and coronets, made of feathers instead of gold and cloth, emblematized their royal status, and their physical difference from Europeans was apparent in their complexions of "olive collour" and hair "blacke and lardge, waving downe to their shoulders." Behind each mounted Indian walked two "Moores, attir'd like *Indian slaves*, that for state sided them," and all were accompanied by torchbearers dressed in Indian garb, "more stravagant than those of the Maskers; all showfully garnisht with several-hewd feathers" (A2ᵛ–A3ʳ).

The procession's display of silver and gold symbolized the English association of the New World with wealth that would enhance the royal power of James I. Along with its feathers and other American signifiers, the pageant also reveals the eclectic theatrical representation of Indians—a quality that persisted for the remainder of the century. Feathers were the most recognizable indication of Indian-ness, but they

An Indian torchbearer; costume design by Inigo Jones for George Chapman's *The Memorable Maske*, 1613.

shared the limelight with bits of East Indian costume ("turbants") and contemporary English dress ("white silke-stockings"). New World natives were often accompanied by young children painted as "Moors," but whereas Indians might appear as priests or princes, black Africans were invariably depicted as subordinates.

When the Phoebades, Chapman's label for Virginian priests, sing three hymns in worship of the setting sun, the second Chorus relates this ritual to James I's imperial enterprise and the royal wedding:

O may our sun not set before,
  he sees his endless seed arise:
And deck his triple crowned shore,
  With springs of humaine Deities.   (D3ᵛ)

Thus the English notion of an empire upon which the sun never sets seems to have started as early as 1613. Having made explicit England's imperial destiny, Chapman then calls for the conversion of the Indians to Christianity, a further symbol of imperial wisdom and power:

> Virginian Princes, ye must now renounce
> Your superstitious worship of these Sunnes,
> Subject to cloudy darknings and descents,
> And of your sweet devotions, turne the events
> To this our Britan *Phoebus*, whose bright skie
> (Enlightened with a Christian Piety)
> Is never subject to black Errors night,
> And hath already offer'd heavens true light,
> To your darke Region; which acknowledge now;
> Descend, and to him all your homage vow.
>
> (D4ᵛ)

The Torchbearers descend and perform a final antimasque in symbolic banishment of disorder and incivility, which, in turn, allows the ladies of the court to join in a dance of heavenly harmony. *The Memorable Maske* ends with an epithalamium, celebrating the royal bride and groom, whose love will usher in "the milke and hony Age." Such aspirations were, of course, as illusionary as the masque itself.

The court masque became even more elaborate during the reign of Charles I. He was oblivious, of course, to the coming civil war that would cost his life, and his court entertainments repeatedly asserted royal control over the forces of disorder. The court masque still symbolized civilizing power, its representations of Indians signifying bestiality and incivility.

Aurelian Townshend's *Tempe Restord*, published in 1632 and designed by Inigo Jones, is a case in point (see cat. no. 63). The antimasque figures who represent vice and bestiality consist of one hare, two hounds, four lions, three apes, six barbarians, five "Hogges," and an ass, as well as "*7 Indians* adoring their Pagode" and "*2 Indians.*"

The beasts (including the barbarians and Indians who "naturally are bestiall") symbolize "that Sensuall desire [which] makes men loose their *Vertue* and Valour, turning Parasites and Slaves to their Bruitish affections."[11] After these antimasquers perform before Circe's court, they are dissolved by Heroic Vertue, who figures "the King Majestie, who therein transcends as farre common men as they are above Beasts, he truly being the prototipe to all the Kingdomes under his Monarchie, of Religion, Justice, and all the *Vertues* joyned together" (p. 104).

Tempe Restord provides a much diminished role for Indians, for here they have lost the beauty and nobility they had enjoyed in Chapman's *Memorable Maske*. Perhaps the novelty of the alien other from the New World had lessened by the 1630s, or perhaps the 1622 massacre of hundreds of Virginia settlers had turned English perceptions strictly toward the "bruitish." At any rate, the Indians in *Tempe Restord* (though still feathered as we see from Inigo Jones's drawing, cat. no. 64) were one-dimensional signifiers of barbarism and incivility.

In 1634 Queen Henrietta and her ladies performed a third Inigo Jones masque, written by William Davenant and staged at Whitehall (see cat. no. 66). *The Temple of Love* reflects English confusion about the world beyond its shores; it conflates characteristics associated with New World natives (especially feathers) with the flora and fauna of East India. The text describes "a naked Indian on a whitish elephant, . . . his tire and bases of several coloured fethers, representing the Indian monarchy." On the other side is an "Asiatique in the habit of an Indian borderer, riding on a camel . . . figured for the Asian monarchy."[12] This seems to be a reference to two of the four continents; if so, the Indian boy represents America, though his elephant certainly came from India.

The text describes the setting for *The Temple of Love* as an "Indian landscape" where strange beasts and birds frolic. In the sea are "several Islands, and afar off a Continent terminating with the horizon." From this sea on a chariot drawn by sea monsters

"Donzella Africana dell'Indie," an African-Indian girl, from Cesare Vecellio, *Habiti antichi et moderni di tutto il mondo* (Venice, 1598). Vecellio was one of Inigo Jones's principal sources for costume ideas, and, like other compilers of costume books, he often confused and conflated elements of the "exotic" cultures.

arrives Indamora, queen of Narsinga (see cat. no. 67). She and her train wear European dress topped with a headdress "with small falls of white feathers tipp'd with watchet" (p. 300). Indamora is instructed by Divine Poesie to reestablish "The Temple of Chaste Love," an allusion to Queen Henrietta's courtly cult of Platonic love. The antimasque in this spectacle seems rather tame; a group of magicians, enemies to Chaste Love, call forth a procession of spirits, who are then banished by Indian priests. The masque concludes when the queen (who portrayed Indamora) and her ladies "begin the Revels with the King and the Lords" (p. 305).

Though she conflates characteristics of East and West, Indamora prefigures the direction theatrical portrayals of Indians would take in the Restoration. Except for the feathers, her clothes are essentially European. The signs of difference—nakedness, olive complexion, long black hair—disappear. Indamora, moreover, is naturally noble and has idealized virtues. Her domain is a golden world, a natural paradise untouched by urban corruption and squalor.[13]

Queen Henrietta's court was doomed. The theatrical extravaganzas she loved so well disappeared from England during the civil war that took her husband's life and did not reappear until her son reclaimed the throne in 1660. Yet the English love of spectacle did not die in the interim. Under the guise of "opera," William Davenant kept theater alive in London, bridging the gap between Caroline court drama and Restoration tragedy. His most famous "opera," *The Siege of Rhodes*, was an elaborate "Representation by the Art of Prospective in Scenes" that depicted Solyman's troops surrounding the ancient city. In 1658 Davenant published the script of a similar "opera," *The Cruelty of the Spaniards in Peru: Exprest by Instrumentall and Vocall Musick, and by Art of Perspective in Scenes, &c.* (see cat. no. 72).

By then England was at war with Spain; the entertainment's main function was to demonize the Spanish and glorify the English, with the people of Peru serving as the instrument. Initially they appear as inhabitants of a golden, innocent age. They wear "feather'd Habits and Bonnets, [and carry] in Indian Baskets, Ingots of Gold and Wedges of Silver," and they partake "in their natural sports of Hunting and Fishing." Perspective scenery portrayed a pastoral habitat, "differing from those of European Climats by representing of Coco-Trees, Pines and Palmitos; and on the boughs of other Trees are seen Munkies, Apes and Parrots; and at farther distance Vallies of Sugar-Canes."[14]

Davenant's opera stresses Indian sun worship and, of course, feathers. For example, the Priest of the Sun appears "cloth'd in a Garment of Feathers longer than any of those that are worn by other Natives" and carries a figure of the sun on his bonnet and dress. After the priest's opening speech, a song depicts the Indians' prelapsarian golden world, "E're crafty Cities made us tame" when "none were rich by bus'ness made." The natives knew no poverty; they hunted and fished; their nakedness provoked no shame, for "all were innocent" (A4ᵛ–B1ᵛ).

Stage engines inaugurated spectacular dances after each of the six scenes. The first entry, for example, concludes with two apes who dance and leap on a rope hanging from the clouds. The second dance occurs after the Incas spy Austrian ships in the harbor and lament the prophecy that "Bearded Peoples" will come to destroy the Inca civilization. The second dance conveys their grief:

> a dolfull Ayre is heard, which prepares the entrance of two Indians, in their feather'd habits of Peru; they enter severally from the opposite sides of the Wood, and gazing on the face of the Scene, fall into a Mimick Dance, in which they express the Argument of the Prospect, by their admiration at the sight of the Ships, (which was to those of Peru a new and wonderfull object) and their lamentation, at beholding their Country-men in deep affliction, and taking their leaves of their wives and Children.   (B3ᵛ)

The destruction of the Inca nation is not solely the Spaniards' responsibility, however, for in a foretaste of Dryden's love tragedies, we are offered an intrigue between two Indian princes; their passionate rivalry proves fatal to orderly succession, leaving the natives easy prey for an invading army.

During the fourth scene of *The Cruelty*, the Spaniards enter and dance a sarabande for the Peruvians, symbolizing their triumph over the Inca nation. The consequences are graphically revealed in a sensational fifth procession aimed at the audience's war fever. The perspective scene opens to a dark prison where "farther to the view are discern'd Racks, and other Engines of torment, with which the Spaniards are tormenting the natives and English Marriners." Davenant then gives his English audience a taste of Spanish atrocities: "Two Spaniards are likewise discover'd, sitting in their cloakes, and appearing more solemn in

ruffs, with Rapiers and Daggers by their sides; the one turning a Spit, whilst the other is basting an Indian prince, which is rosted in an artificiall fire" (C4ʳ). All is not lost, however, for the final entry displays the English army in the distance, wearing "Red-Coats." Davenant admits to his readers that this scene "may seem improper, because the English had made no discovery of Peru, in the time of the Spaniards first invasion there." But, he argues, this anachronicity is appropriate in "Poeticall Representations of this nature"; it may pass as a "Vision discern'd by the Priest of the Sun" whose prophecy foretells "the subversion of the Spaniards by the English" (D3ʳ–D4ᵛ) — presumably by Cromwell's army. The final dance concludes with the English and Indians saluting and shaking hands.

In Davenant's panorama of Spanish cruelties, the principal purpose of New World peoples is to signify English ascendancy in the struggle with Spain. His pageant also demonstrates that by the middle of the 17th century the simple display of Indians (signified by feathers) no longer evoked wonder and delight. Davenant relied on perspective scenery, music, and dances to enthrall his audience; Indians were peripheral.

After the Restoration John Dryden picked up where Davenant had left off. Although Sir Robert Howard was partly responsible for *The Indian-Queen* (1664), Dryden wrote most of the text, which was lavishly mounted by the King's Company at the Theatre Royal (see cat. no. 74). The costumes were also spectacular; the Indian queen's garb was decked with wreaths of feathers from Suriname, contributed by Aphra Behn.[15] The play depicts the Indian kingdom as a natural paradise until internal dissension weakens the state. Written nearly 150 years after the events it purports to represent, *The Indian-Queen* takes incredible liberties with history. Montezuma, a general in the Peruvian army, serves "the Inca," the Peruvian king, yet later Montezuma is revealed to be the lawful heir to the kingdom of Mexico.

The Indian-Queen follows the conventional pattern of heroic tragedy by featuring noble young men who begin as friends but become rivals in love. Intrigue abounds. Montezuma is paired with Acacis, son of the usurping Mexican queen, Zempoalla. Whereas Montezuma is characterized as overly passionate, Acacis is a man of reason. Although the text is not overtly propagandistic, as Davenant's opera had been, Montezuma's natural nobility and his insistence on royal prerogatives reflects Dryden's strong monarchist stance.

Dryden uses spectacle to represent Indian culture. Though she is a usurper, the Indian queen appears with all the feathered pomp and circumstance the King's Company could muster. The opening of act 3, for example, reads:

> Zempoalla *appears seated upon her Slaves in Triumph, attended by* Traxalla; *and the* Indians *as to celebrate the Victory, advance in a warlike Dance; in the midst of which Triumph,* Acacis *and* Montezuma *fall in upon them.*[16]

Later, when the fortunes of war reverse, Montezuma is captured and prepared for sacrifice. Here we have late-17th-century England's conception of Aztec rites: *"The Scene opens, and discovers the Temple of the Sun all of Gold, and four Priests in habits of white and red Feathers attending by a bloody Altar, as ready for sacrifice"* (p. 220). Before Montezuma's dismemberment can take place, however, Acacis, the Indian who represents Dryden's rational man, rebukes the assembled worshipers:

> Hold, hold, such sacrifices cannot be
> Devotion's, but a solemn cruelty:
> How can the Gods delight in humane blood?
> Think 'um not cruel; if you think 'um good.
> In vain we ask that mercy which they want,
> And hope that pitty which they hate to grant.
>
> (p. 223)

The Indian-Queen concludes with the defeat of Zempoalla, the revelation that Montezuma was spirited away at birth and raised in obscurity because he was the legitimate heir to the Mexican throne, and his joyful betrothal to Orazia, Peruvian daughter to the Inca. In the epilogue, Montezuma admits that the Indians would rather face the Spanish than caustic theater critics:

> You have seen all that this old World cou'd do,
> We therefore try the fortunes of the new,

Montezuma, from John Ogilby, *America* (London, 1671).

> And hope it is below your aim to hit
> An untaught nature with your practic'd Wit.
>
> (p. 231)

Thus the "naked Indians" differ from Europeans in their "untaught" simplicity. As presented by Howard and Dryden, however, their complex emotional negotiations between sexual passion and heroic valor seem positively European.

Montezuma need not have worried about the critics. *The Indian-Queen* was such a success that two years later Dryden prepared a sequel, *The Indian Emperour* (see cat. no. 76). The same scenes and costumes were used, and the plot, extended to Montezuma's and Zempoalla's sons and daughters, is much the same. What makes *The Indian Emperour* particularly interesting is the frame: Dryden claims in the dedicatory epistle to Princess Anne that Montezuma's *"story is, perhaps the greatest, which was ever represented in a Poem of this Nature; (the action of it including the Discovery and Conquest of a New World.)"*[17] Dryden's lovers and fighters cavort before this momentous backdrop: Cortés's arrival, the siege of Tenochtitlán, the destruction of the Aztec civilization, and finally, Montezuma's death.

Because the conquerors were Spanish, not English, the play is frequently sympathetic to the Indians and critical of the conquerors. The resulting clash of cultures is ambiguous. There are virtuous heroes and villainous cheats on both sides, and the cultures themselves have mixtures of good and evil. Dryden implies throughout that, despite their sacrificial rites, the Indians' natural nobility is superior to European cruelty and corruption, a view he no doubt adapted from Montaigne.[18]

The play begins with Vasquez, a greedy Spaniard, who lays bare his ethnocentrism:

Corn,[19] Wine, and Oyl are wanting to this
      ground,
In which our Countries fruitfully abound:
As if this Infant world, yet un-array'd,
Naked and bare, in Natures Lap were laid.
No useful Arts have yet found footing here;
But all untaught and salvage does appear.   (p. 1)

Cortés, a more sympathetic character, argues that difference does not necessarily mean inferiority:

Wild and untaught are Terms which we alone
Invent, for fashions differing from our own:
For all their Customs are by Nature wrought,
But we, by Art, unteach what Nature taught.

(p. 1)

Vasquez's Spanish jingoism is undercut when Montezuma replies from a perspective suspiciously similar to the English viewpoint:

You speak your Prince a mighty Emperour,
But his demands have spoke him Proud, and
      Poor;
. . . But, by what right pretends your King to be
This Soveraign Lord of all the World, and me?

Montezuma's inability to accept Vasquez's demands clearly stems from wisdom, not from ignorance.

After all, he argues, "He who Religion truely understands / Knows its extent must be in Men, not Lands" (p. 11).

Whatever their moral failings, the Spanish are superior in technology. Montezuma's second son, Guyomar, describes the Indian reaction to Spanish armor:

I fell'd along a Man of Bearded face,
His limbs all cover'd with a Shining case:
So wonderous hard, and so secure of wound,
It made my Sword, though edged with Flint,
      rebound.   (p. 21)

If armor and guns give the Spanish an advantage, cowardice and valor co-exist on both sides.

The Indian Emperour depicts the siege of the Aztec capital, the people's starvation, and the destruction of the empire. Determined to uncover Aztec gold, Pizarro and a Christian priest torture Montezuma on the rack. Suffering by his side is an Indian priest who speculates about Christian hypocrisy: "Can Heaven be Author of such Cruelty?" Pizarro responds with more torture, but despite the pain, Montezuma remains steadfast, arguing for a "middle way" as opposed to Catholic extremes. In frustration, Pizarro exclaims, "Increase their Pains, the Cords are yet too Slack." The Christian priest complies, "I must by force, convert him on the Rack" (p. 60). Once again, English representations of the Indians are a powerful vehicle for anti-Spanish, anti-Catholic propaganda.

Dryden's Cortés, unlike his fellows, is an honorable and merciful man. He stops the torture and offers Montezuma his life; the hero refuses and, protesting his resolution to die freely, stabs himself. *The Indian Emperour* concludes in the exalted tones of heroic tragedy, but the hero's fall guarantees the destruction of the nation. The Aztecs will follow the slain hero's son, Guyomar, into banishment:

Northward, beyond the Mountains we will go,
Where Rocks lye cover'd with Eternal Snow;
Thin Herbage in the Plains, and Fruitless Fields,
The Sand no Gold, the Mine no Silver yields:
There Love and Freedom we'll in Peace enjoy;
No *Spaniards* will that Colony destroy.   (p. 68)

In northern climes the Indians will, presumably, be able to reestablish their golden world, for if they encounter Europeans, it will be the benign English, rather than the cruel and rapacious Spanish.

Dryden's representations of Indians were remote in time and space from his audience's experience. Aphra Behn, by contrast, had actually been in Suriname, and her play, *The Widdow Ranter* (1688), is a more realistic presentation of English experience in the New World (see cat. no. 79). Set in the Virginia colony at the time of Bacon's Rebellion (1676), the play mixes a comic plot with the tragic story of Nathaniel Bacon's aborted attempt to overthrow the royal government. The historical Bacon attacked Indians with little discrimination, then exploited his popularity in a confrontation with the governor, Sir William Berkeley. The Indian fighter captured Jamestown for a time, but after his sudden death, colonial authority was reimposed and the tidewater aristocracy remained in power.

Though the play's tone is pro-Bacon and pro-English, it at least mentions English responsibility for the Indians' plight. A newcomer is informed that "the *Indians* by our ill Management of Trade, whom we have Armed against Our selves, Very frequently make War upon us with our own Weapons, Tho' often coming by the Worst are forced to make Peace with us again, but so, as upon every turn they fall to Massacring us wherever we ly exposed to them."[20]

Behn's comic banter is set against the discourse of heroic tragedy when Bacon falls in love with Semernia, the Indian queen. She is married to a noble king, who addresses Bacon as an equal:

> For your part, Sir, you've been so Noble, that I repent the fatall difference that makes us meet in Arms. Yet tho' I'm young I'm sensible of Injuries; And oft have heard my Grandsire say—that we were Monarchs once of all this spacious World; Till you an unknown People landing here, Distress'd and ruin'd by destructive storms, Abusing all our Charitable Hospitality, Usurp'd our Right, and made your friends your slaves. (p. 13)

The Indian queen begs Bacon to spare her people and make peace. Before Bacon can secure her

A mezzotint portrait by William Vincent, c. 1700, of the actress Anne Bracegirdle, who first played the role of the Indian queen in Aphra Behn's *The Widdow Ranter*.

desires (and her love), he is ambushed by the Virginia council's men and declared a traitor. The Indians, convinced of English treachery, prepare for war:

> *A Temple, with an* Indian *God placed upon it, Priests and Priestesses attending; Enter* Indian *King on one side attended by* Indian *Men, the Queen Enters on the other side with Women, all bow to the Idol, and divide on each side of the Stage, then the Musick Playing lowder, the Priest and Priestesses Dance about the Idol, with ridiculous Postures and Crying (as for Incantations). Thrice repeated,* Agah Yerkin, Agah Boah, Sulen Tawarapah, Sulen Tawarapah. (p. 36)

One can only speculate whether this scene resembles anything Behn had observed in Suriname or was merely inserted to please the groundlings. Nevertheless, after much more of this sort of hocus-pocus, the Priest prophesies that Bacon will be captured and the Indians' only recourse is to fight. The English, in turn, suddenly realize the Indian threat and release Bacon, who kills the

Indian king in a man-to-man encounter. In the play's final scene, the queen enters dressed *"like an Indian Man, with a Bow in her hand and Quiver at her Back"* (p. 50). She is soon wounded, however, and rather than live without her, Bacon takes poison, thereby ending the rebellion.

In *The Widdow Ranter* Aphra Behn combines heroic love trappings with a comparatively realistic awareness of the complexities of English colonization and, perhaps, a hint or two that English policy toward the Indians just might be wrongheaded and unfair. Her Indians are no worse and no better than their English counterparts; some are noble, some are base. When they lose their king, they are doomed, just as the stout yeomen who follow Bacon are destroyed by his demise.

The final play in this survey is Thomas Southerne's *Oroonoko*, a tragedy based on Aphra Behn's novel of the same name (see cat. no. 77). Indians play a relatively insignificant role in this play, for the focus shifts from first encounters and frontier relationships to the importation of black slaves from Africa. Southerne follows Behn's novel fairly closely but adds a comic plot complete with a "breeches role" (a part that demanded crossdressing, thereby allowing actresses to display their shapely legs) to leaven the seriousness of Oroonoko's tragic fate. The Indians' principal role in act 2, scene 3, is a revolt against the colonists quelled by the black slave Oroonoko:

> *A Party of* Indians *enter, hurrying* Imoinda [Oroonoko's beloved wife] *among the Slaves; another Party of* Indians *sustains 'em retreating, follow'd at a distance by the Governour with the Planters.*[21]

Oroonoko, a prince among his own people, is perhaps a prototype of the noble savage, true to his love and his own integrity. His natural virtues expose the corruption of European powers: the English merchant Blandford pronounces this epitaph over Oroonoko's body in the play's closing lines:

> I hope there is a place of Happiness
> In the next World for such exalted Virtue.
> Pagan, or Unbeliever, yet he liv'd
> To all he knew; And if he went astray,

> There's Mercy still above to set him right.
> But Christians guided by the Heavenly Ray,
> Have no excuse if we mistake our way.   (p. 84)

Oroonoko represents a heroic treatment of the second stage of England's colonial enterprise—full settlement, the near-destruction of the Indians, and the importation of African slaves to work large and remunerative plantations.

Southerne's casual insertion of an Indian rebellion in the middle of his play suggests that times had changed since Indians were first represented on the British stage. The strangeness had almost wholly worn off; no longer were Indians sources of wonder and delight. As the British empire changed from an aspiration to a reality, Indians ceased to symbolize England's destiny. As English settlement intensified along the eastern seaboard of North America, Indians became farther removed from cities and towns; accordingly they receded from center stage in the unfolding American drama and its English representation to become merely a theatrical backdrop.

Virginia Mason Vaughan is Professor of English, Clark University, Worcester, Massachusetts

Notes

1. See Stephen Greenblatt, *Marvelous Possessions: The Wonder of the New World* (Oxford: Clarendon Press, 1991), p. 14.

2. Hugh Honour, *The New Golden Land: European Images of America from the Discoveries to the Present Time* (New York: Pantheon Books, 1975), p. 26.

3. See Alden T. Vaughan and Virginia Mason Vaughan, *Shakespeare's Caliban: A Cultural History* (Cambridge: Cambridge University Press, 1991), pp. 43–50, for a discussion of Caliban's Indian-ness.

4. George Chapman, *Eastward Ho!*, ed. R. W. van Fossen (Baltimore: Johns Hopkins University Press, 1979), p. 138. Fossen notes that Seagull's history is faulty, since the first English colony in Virginia was not settled until 1585. Seagull may be alluding to the lost colony of Roanoke, which disappeared without a trace in the late 1580s.

5. André Thevet, *The New Found Worlde, or Antarctike*, trans. T. Hacket (London: by Henrie Bynneman for T. Hacket, 1568), p. [45].

6. Jean Ribaut, quoted in *Discovering the New World (based on the works of Theodore de Bry)*, ed. Michael Alexander (New York: Harper and Row, 1976), p. 12.

7. Michel de Montaigne, *The Essayes: or Morall, Politike and Millitarie Discourses*, trans. John Florio (London: by Val. Sims for Edward Blount, 1603), pp. 100–107.

8. Stephen Orgel and Roy Strong, *Inigo Jones: The Theatre of the Stuart Court* (Berkeley: University of California Press, 1973), p. 50.

9. Stephen Orgel, *The Illusion of Power: Political Theater in the Renaissance* (Berkeley: University of California Press, 1975), p. 39.

10. George Chapman, *The Memorable Maske* (London: by G. Eld for George Norton, 1613), sig. A1ᵛ. Citations from this masque will be indicated by signature numbers in parentheses.

11. Aurelian Townshend, *Tempe Restored*, in *The Poems and Masques of Aurelian Townshend*, ed. Cedric C. Brown (Reading, England: Whiteknights Press, 1983), p. 104.

12. William Davenant, *The Works of D'avenant*, ed. James Maidment and W. H. Logan (Edinburgh and London: William Paterson and Sotheran & Co., 1872), vol. 1, p. 287.

13. See Honour, *New Golden Land*, p. 6, for a discussion of the explorers' superimposition of ancient Rome's "golden age" onto the lands and peoples they discovered.

14. William Davenant, *The Cruelty of the Spaniards in Peru* (London: for Henry Herringman, 1658), sigs. A3ʳ–A3ᵛ.

15. See Eugene M. Waith, *Ideas of Greatness: Heroic Drama in England* (London: Routledge and Kegan Paul, 1971), p. 206.

16. John Dryden, *The Works of John Dryden*, vol. 8, ed. John Harrington Smith and Dougald MacMillan (Berkeley: University of California Press, 1962), p. 201. Subsequent citations will be noted by page number in the text.

17. John Dryden, *The Indian Emperour; or, The Conquest of Mexico by the Spaniards*, 2d ed. (London: for H. Herringman, 1668), sigs. C1ʳ–C1ᵛ.

18. See the editors' commentary in *Works of Dryden*, vol. 9, pp. 310–316, for an analysis of Dryden's debt to Montaigne.

19. "Corn" in this context refers to European wheat.

20. Aphra Behn, *The Widdow Ranter; or, The History of Bacon in Virginia* (London: for James Knapton, 1690), p. 3.

21. Thomas Southerne, *Oroonoko: A Tragedy* (London: for H. Playford, 1696), p. 31.

"En la mode des sauvages
de l'Amérique"

C'est la Deduction du sumptueux ordre plaisantz spectacles, 1551

Many of the American Indians transported to Europe from the 15th
century onward were put on display—introduced at court or paraded
at fairs or in public processions. A few were incorporated into elaborate
public pageants celebrating royal entries or weddings. As Europe's
awareness of the New World grew, however, such pageantry often
included Europeans themselves, dressed in feather skirts and headdresses to represent Indians. Sometimes the "Indian" attire was fantastic, bearing no relationship to reality but serving, nevertheless, to
incorporate the "exotic" areas of the world into the festivities. "Americans" and symbols of America were included in numerous 16th- and
17th-century ceremonial royal entries (see Mullaney, "The New
World on Display," above).

Figure des Brisilians.

54 *C'est la Deduction du sumptueux ordre plaisantz*
     spectacles et Magnifiques Theatres . . . Exhibes
     Par Les Citoiens de Rouen . . . A . . . Henry
     second . . . et . . . Katharine de Medicis

     Rouen, Jean Le Prest, 1551
     Shelf mark: DC 114.3 C4 1551 Cage

In 1550 a meadow on the outskirts of Rouen was turned into a "Brazilian forest" where two Brazilian villages were constructed "in true native fashion." Over 50 Tupinamba Indians were imported to occupy this Brazilian landscape along with some 250 Frenchmen who were costumed as Tupinamba. The occasion was the royal entry into Rouen of Henri II and Catherine de Médicis. This most thorough performance of a New World culture is described in some detail by Mullaney, "The New World on Display," above.

ARCVS LVSITANORVM .

55   Jean Boch (1555–1609)
      Descriptio Publicae Gratulationis, Spectaculorum
      et Ludorum in Adventu . . . Ernesti Archiducis
      Austriae
          Antwerp, Ex officina Plantiniana, 1595
          Shelf mark: ac 222738
          The Gift of Mrs. H. Dunscombe Colt

In 1594 Ernest, archduke of Austria, made his formal entry into the city of Antwerp as its new governor. The city put on a lavish display for him,
following many of the traditions associated with
the royal entries of sovereigns. Proceeding along
a fixed route, the new governor passed under
triumphal arches designed by Marten de Vos,

Antwerp's leading painter. The event was com-
memorated in a book by Jean Boch with engravings by Pieter van der Borcht. The Arch of the
Lusitanians, or Portuguese, publicized Portugal's colonial empire. The figure of Poseidon at the
top of the arch was a reminder that Portugal made
its conquests by sea. Emblematic figures represented Portugal's empires in Africa (Mauretania,
Ethiopia), India, and the New World (Brasilia).
The female figure representing Brazil wears a
feather skirt and rides an armadillo. She carries an
arrow and club in one hand and a severed foot in
the other, all symbols of Brazilian culture and
customs as understood by the Europeans.

56   Johann Gaspard Gevaerts (1593–1666)
      *Pompa Introitus Honori Serenissimi Principis
      Ferdinandi . . . a . . . Antverp, Decreta*
      Antwerp, Joannes Meursius, 1642
      Shelf mark: ac 209225

Another triumphal arch incorporating symbols of
the New World was the Arch of the Mint designed
by Rubens and Johann Gaspard Gevaerts for the
1634 entry of Prince Ferdinand, brother of Philip
IV, into Antwerp as the new Spanish governor of
the Netherlands. The artists may have been partly
inspired by the title page of de Bry's *Americae pars*

sexta with its illustration of Mount Potosí, the
richest silver mine in the world. The Arch of the
Mint, constructed in the form of a mountain
intended to represent Mount Potosí, was commem-
orated, like the rest of the street decorations, in
engravings by Theodor van Thulden after Rubens's
designs. Its combination of classical and New
World imagery and the contrasting moods of the
two sides of the arch are discussed by Mullaney,
"The New World on Display," above.

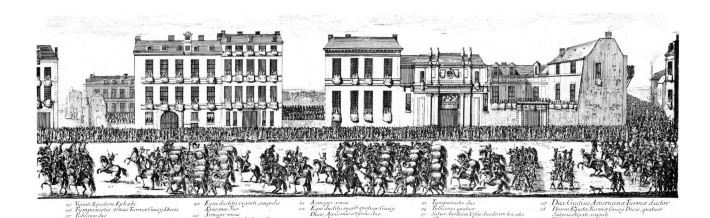

57   Charles Perrault (1628–1703)
Festiva ad Capita Annulumque Decursio, a Rege Ludovico XIV

Paris, Sebastian Mabre-Cramoisy, 1670
Shelf mark: DC 126 P4 L3 1670 Cage

In 1662 Louis XIV staged one of the most elaborate public festivities of all time, a tournament, or carousel, held near the Louvre in a space which has since been named La Place du Carrousel. Members of the court were dressed in costumes representing five nations: Romans (led by Louis himself), Persians, Turks, Indians (presumably from India), and "Americans." Although they appear to have been covered with feathers, the tympanist and trumpeter of "America" bear no resemblance to any of the Native Americans who were seen in Europe and depicted by artists of the period. The duc de Guise, billed as the American king, wore an elaborate feather headdress, but he was dressed in "dragon skin" and rode a "unicorn" decorated with serpents. Other Americans were dressed as savages, wearing leaves and carrying crude clubs, and one of the lance bearers had an opossum on his helmet.

"All Showfully Garnisht with Several-Hewd Fethers"

George Chapman, *The Memorable Maske*, 1613

Royal weddings were occasions for elaborate public festivities, some lasting for several days. Tournaments, pageants, and processions, all with lavish and often fantastic costumes, promoted the ruling families' union through marriage. These were times when a monarch's public could witness the splendor of his court, and when representatives from around the world could participate in the festivities. The inclusion of actual representatives of "exotic" or alien cultures, as at Rouen in 1550, was uncommon. More often, participants in the pageantry "represented" those other cultures with varying degrees of accuracy.

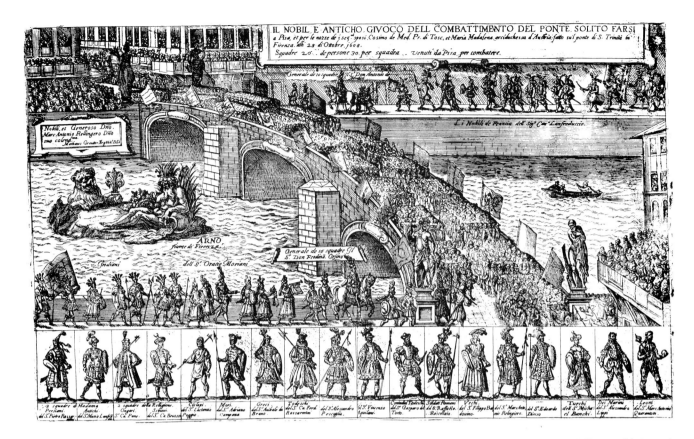

58   Camillo Rinuccini (1564–1649)
*Descrizione Delle Feste Fatte Nelle Reali Nozze
de' . . . D. Cosimo de' Medici, e Maria
Maddalena Arciduchessa d'Austria*

Florence, Appresso i Giunti, 1608
Shelf mark: DG 738.23 R5 1608a Cage

Festivities celebrating the marriage of Cosimo de'
Medici II to Maria Magdalena of Austria in 1608
continued an entire month. On the eleventh day,
the people of Florence witnessed a mock battle
staged on the Santa Trinità bridge, during which a
group of noblemen from Pisa fought and defeated
warriors from "every foreign land." Examples
ranging from Roman centurions to contemporary
Moors are depicted along the bottom of Matthias
Greuter's engraving of the event. On the banks of
the river is a group of American Indians in the
usual feather skirts and headdresses.

Der Ander Auffzug zum Carisell.

59   Balthasar Küchler (1571?–1641)

Repraesentatio der Fürstlichen Auffzug und Ritterspil. So bei des . . . Herrn Johann Friderichen Hertzogen zu Württenberg . . . und der . . . Barbara Sophien geborne Marggravin zu Brandenburgi Hochzeitlich . . . 1609.

     [N.p., 1611]
     Shelf mark: 222-707f
     The Gift of Mrs. H. Dunscombe Colt

Over 200 engravings by Balthasar Küchler depict the festivities for the marriage of Johann Friedrich, prince of Württemberg, and Barbara Sophia, margravine of Brandenburg, in 1609. Five plates show mounted musicians and warriors decorated with tattoos and wearing feather skirts. The skirts, made of several layers of feathers, are typical of 17th-century stage conventions for representing Indians and are not accurate representations of the Tupinamba skirts that probably inspired them. The tattooing may have been copied from some of the de Bry engravings of Florida Indians, whereas the horns, shields, and bows and arrows are European. The source for the helmets is unknown.

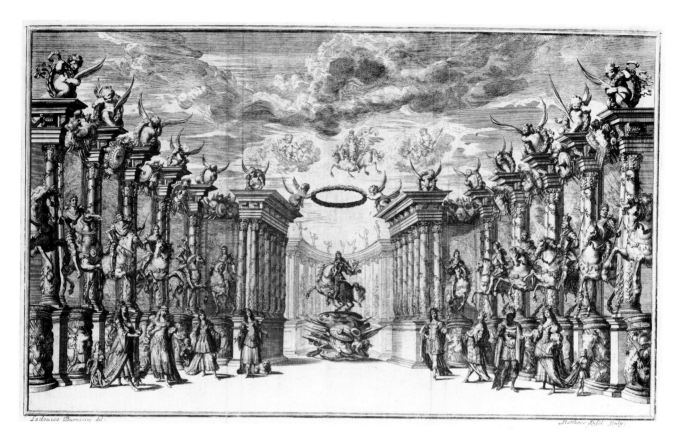

60   Francesco Sbarra (17th cent.)
      *Il Pomo d'Oro, Festa Teatrale Rappresentata in
      Vienna per . . . Nozze . . . di Leopoldo, e
      Margherita*

      Vienna, Matteo Cosmerovio, 1668
      Shelf mark: PQ 4634 S228 P7 1668 Cage

Celebrations for the marriage of Emperor Leopold I
to Margherita Theresa of Spain included a performance of Francesco Sbarra's *Il Pomo d'Oro*. The play
itself, performed on this occasion with ornate and
elaborately detailed stage settings, was based on
the classical story of the golden apple. The pro-
logue, however, glorified Austria with a setting
that included equestrian statues of all its emperors.
At the front were two choruses, one representing the Holy Roman Empire and the kingdoms
of Hungary, Italy, and Sardinia, and the other,
Spain, America, the kingdom of Bohemia, and
Germany. America, with his feather headdress, is
noticeably dark-skinned.

"Altogether Estrangfull, and *Indian* Like"

George Chapman, *The Memorable Maske*, 1613

Although New World natives were seen in London as early as 1502, when Sebastian Cabot presented three people from Newfoundland to the court of Henry VII, "Indians" did not appear in the English popular theater or in court masques until after the Roanoke expeditions of the 1580s. As the English began to establish settlements in America, and as printed illustrations of Indians became more common, the writers and producers of masques performed at the Stuart court introduced strangely garbed Indians, with "ruffes of feathers" and skin of "olive collour," into their festivities. Feathers were generally the indication of Indian-ness, as gold and silver were reminders of the New World's wealth. In these court entertainments, which included music and dance, the spectacle and the disguises donned by members of the court were usually more important than the plot. Indians were often part of the antimasque, serving as symbols of disorder (see Vaughan, "Salvages and Men of Ind," above). The architect Inigo Jones designed the settings, machinery, and costumes for many of the masques.

THE
MEMORABLE MASKE

of the two Honorable Houses or Inns of
Court ; the Middle Temple, and
Lyncolns Inne.

As it was performd before the King, at
White-Hall on Shroue Munday at night;
being the 15. of February. 1613.

At the Princely celebration of the moft Royall
Nuptialls of the Palſgraue, *and his thrice gratious
Princeſſe* Elizabeth.&c.

With a deſcription of their whole ſhow; in the manner
of their march on horſe-backe to the Court from
the Maiſter of the Rolls his houſe : with all
*their right Noble conſorts, and moſt
ſhowfull attendants.*

Inuented, and faſhioned, with the ground, and
ſpeciall ſtructure of the whole worke,

By our Kingdomes moſt Artfull and Ingenious
Architect INNIGO IONES.

Supplied, Aplied, Digeſted, and written,
By GEO: CHAPMAN.

AT LONDON,
Printed by *G. Eld* , for *George Norton* and are to be
ſould at his ſhoppe neere Temple-bar.

61   George Chapman (1559?–1634)
     The Memorable Maske of the two Honorable
     Houses or Inns of Court; the Middle Temple,
     and Lyncolns Inne

          London, G. Eld for George Norton, [1613?]
          Shelf mark: STC 4981

The Memorable Maske was performed in celebration
of the marriage in 1613 of Princess Elizabeth to
Frederick V, Elector Palatine. The masque was
organized by the Gentlemen of the Inns of Court,
some of whom had invested in the Virginia Company and wanted royal patronage for their venture. Inigo Jones provided the designs, and the performance took place at the palace at Whitehall
on February 15, 1613. The masque began with
a procession of antimasque figures, including
"Baboons." They were followed by "the choice
Musitions of our Kingdome" costumed as Virginian priests adoring the sun, with "strange Hoods
of feathers . . . and . . . turbants, stucke with severall colour'd feathers." The "chiefe Maskers"
were also in "Indian habits . . . richly embroidered, with golden Sunns . . . like the Virginian
Princes they presented . . . Altogether estrangfull
and *Indian* like." Torchbearers were dressed in
Indian garb "more stravagant then those of the
Maskers; all showfully garnisht with several-hewd
fethers." (For further discussion of this masque,
see Vaughan, "Salvages and Men of Ind," above.)

Temple, and Lincolns Inne.

the number of a hundred.

     The Torch-bearers habits were likewise of
the *Indian* garb, but more ftrauagant then
thofe of the Maskers; all fhowfully garnifht
with feueral-hewd fethers. The humble variety whereof, ftucke off the more amplie, the
Maskers high beauties, fhining in the habits
of themfelues; and reflected in their kinde,
a new and delightfully-varied radiance on
the beholders.

     All thefe fuftaind torches of *Virgine* wax,
whofe ftaues were great canes al ouer gilded;
And thefe (as the reft) had euery Man his
Moore, attending his horfe.

     The Maskers, riding fingle; had euery
Masker, his Torch-bearer mounted before
him.

     The laft Charriot, which was moft of all
adornd; had his whole frame fill'd with moul-
ded worke; mixt all with paintings, and
glittering fcarffings of filuer; ouer which was
caft a Canopie of golde, boarne vp with an-
tick figures, and all compos'd *a la Grotefea.*
Before this in the feate of it, as the Chario-
                                        tere;

62   Inigo Jones (1573–1652)
      An Indian Torchbearer
          Pen, brown ink, and watercolor
          28.6 × 16.1 cm
          Lent by the duke of Devonshire and the
          Chatsworth Settlement Trustees

Jones's torchbearer, "garnisht with several-hewd fethers," is undoubtedly based on published costume books of the period. In *Inigo Jones: The Theatre of the Stuart Court* (1973), Stephen Orgel and Roy Strong suggest that Jones's inspiration was the figure of Indo Africano, which appeared in Cesare Vecellio's *Habiti antichi et moderni di tutto il mondo* (Venice, 1598), the source Jones used most frequently. Among the expenses for the masque, in the records of the Honourable Society of Lincoln's Inn, is a payment "to Mr. Roberte Johnes, haberdasher, for fethers and trimminge of suites and head attires, £190."

63   Aurelian Townshend (fl. 1601–1643)
      Tempe Restord: A Masque Presented by the
      Queene, and foureteene Ladies
          London, A. M. for Robert Allet and
          George Bake[r], 1631 [1632]
          Shelf mark: STC 24156

The court entertainments of Charles I were even more elaborate than those of James I and were used repeatedly to assert royal control over forces of disorder. Among the antimasque figures in *Tempe Restord* were "7 Indians adoring their Pagole [pagoda]," one idol, one hare, two hounds, four lions, three apes, six barbarians, five hogs, and an ass. The beasts, including the Indians and barbarians, "who naturally are bestiall," symbolize "that Sensuall desire [which] makes men loose their *Vertue* and Valour, turning Parasites and Slaves to their Brutish affections." The role of the Indians in this masque is a much diminished one, and they have lost their nobility. Perhaps the 1622 massacre of hundreds of settlers in Virginia had changed English perceptions of the Indians.

TEMPE
RESTORD.

A Masque

Presented by the QVEENE, and foureteene Ladies, to the KINGS MAIESTIE at *Whitehall* on Shrove-Tuesday.
1631.

LONDON:
Printed by *A. M.* for ROBERT ALLET,
and GEORGE BAKER.
1631.

(7)

Circe. Then take my keyes ! and shew me al my wealth:
Leade me abroad ! Let me my subiects view!
Bring me some Physick! though that bring no health!
And feyne me pleasures, since I finde none true.

Chorus.

Yee willing Servants ! And ye Soules confin'd
To severall shapes, by powerfull Herbes and Art,
Appeare, transform'd each in your severall kind,
And striue to temper the distemper'd Heart,
Of sullen Circe, stung with Cupids dart.

Her song ended, she sits, and before her are presented all the Antimasques, consisting of Indians, and Barbarians, who naturally are bestiall, and others which are voluntaries, and but halfe transformed into beastes.

Here come forth all the Anti-masques.

 7. *Indians adoring their*
  Pagole.
 1. *Idoll.*
 1. *Hare.*
 2. *Hounds.*
 4. *Lyons.*
 3. *Apes.*

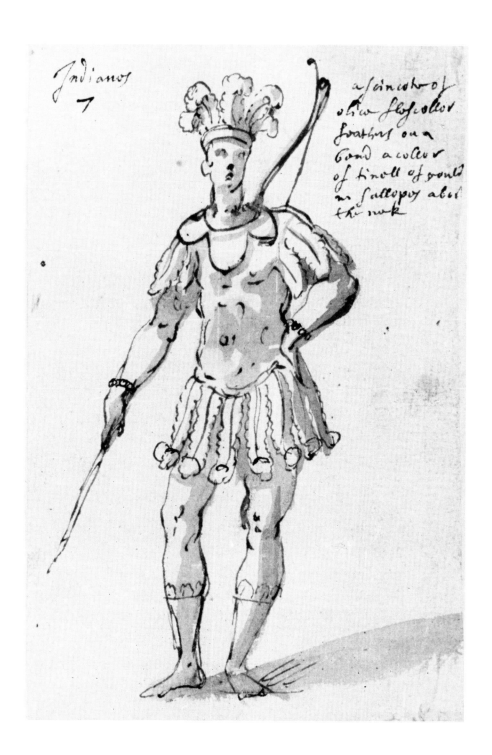

64   Inigo Jones (1573–1652)
      Indians, for *Tempe Restord*
          Pen and brown ink washed with gray
          16.9 × 11.2 cm
          Lent by the duke of Devonshire and the
          Chatsworth Settlement Trustees

Jones based the costumes for the "Indians" on those in Matthias Greuter's engraving of the mock battle staged in 1608 for the wedding of Cosimo de' Medici II (see cat. no. 58). The inscription on the right-hand side of the drawing reads, "a scincote of / olive fleshcollor / feathers on a bend a collor / of tin[s]ell of gould / in s[c]allopes about / the neck."

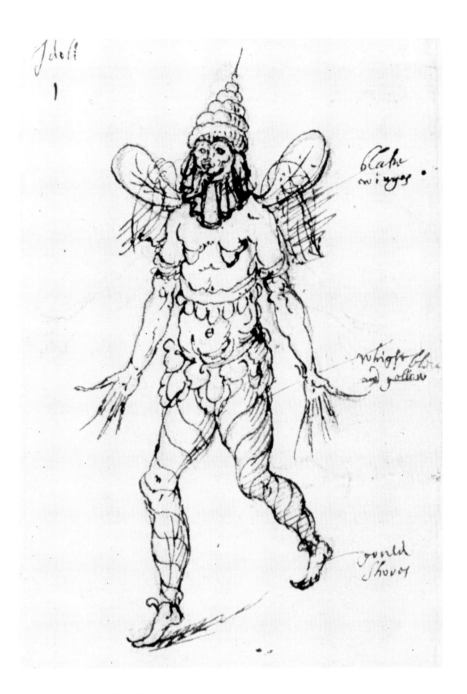

65   Inigo Jones (1573–1652)
      Idoll

        Pen and brown ink
        16.7 × 11.4 cm
        Lent by the duke of Devonshire and the
        Chatsworth Settlement Trustees

In *The Memorable Maske*, feathers were the principal indication of Indian-ness, but elements of the East crept into the costumes in the "turbants" stuck with feathers. Here again, in the *Idoll*, Eastern elements seem dominant, probably because Townshend described the Indians as "adoring their Pagole [pagoda]." There is little resemblance, for instance, to the idols depicted in either Harriot's *Briefe and true report*, 1590, or Robert Vaughan's engraving for Smith's *Generall Historie of Virginia* (1624; cat. no. 22).

THE
TEMPLE
OF
LOVE.

A Masque.

Prefented by the QVEENES Ma-
jefty, and her Ladies, at *White-hall* on
Shrove-Tuefday, 1634.

By *Inigo Iones*, Surveyor of his Ma[ties.] Workes,
and *William Davenant*, her Ma[ties.] Servant.

S[y] First Edition.

LONDON:

Printed for *Thomas Walkley*, and are to be fold at his
Shop neare *White-hall.* 1634.

66   Sir William Davenant (1606–1668)
   The Temple of Love: A Masque Presented by the Queenes Majesty, and her Ladies
   London, for Thomas Walkley, 1634 [1635]
   Shelf mark: STC 14719

More than either *The Memorable Maske* or *Tempe Restord*, *The Temple of Love* reflects English confusion about Indians and the world they inhabited. It conflates New World characteristics such as feathers with the flora and fauna of the East. The text describes "a naked Indian on a whitish elephant, . . . his tire and bases of several coloured fethers, representing the Indian monarchy." The setting for the masque is described as an "Indian landscape" with strange birds and beasts. In the sea are "several Islands, and afar off a Continent terminating with the horizon." Indamora, Queen of Narsinga, arrives from the sea on a chariot drawn by sea monsters. She wears a European dress topped with a headdress "with small falls of white feathers." As her name may indicate (a combination of Indian and Moor), Indamora combines characteristics of East and West, but she also indicates the direction theatrical portrayals of Indians would take in the Restoration. Except for the feathers, her costume is European. She is innately noble and her world is a golden one, a natural paradise.

THE TEMPLE
OF LOVE.

AT the lower end of the Banquetting-houfe, oppofite to the State, was a Stage of fix foot high, and on that was raifed an Ornament of a new Invention agreeable to the Subject; confifting of Indian Trophees: on the one fide upon a bafement fate a naked Indian on a whitifh Elephant, his legges fhortning towards the necke of the beaft, his tire and bafes of feverall coloured feathers, reprefenting the Indian Monarchy: On the other fide an Afiatique in the habit of an Indian borderer, riding on a Camell; his Turbant and Coat differing from that of the Turkes, figured for the Afian Monarchy: over thefe hung fheild like Compartiments: In that over the Indian was painted a Sunne rifing, and in the other an halfe Moone; thefe had for finifhing the Capitall of a great pillafter, which ferved as a ground to fticke them of, and bore up a large freeze or border with a Coronice. In this over the Indian lay the figure of an old man, with a long white haire and beard, reprefenting the flood *Tigris*; on his head a wreath of Canes and Seage, and leaning upon a great Vrne, out of which runne water, by him in an extravagant pofture ftood a Tyger.

At the other end of this freeze lay another naked man, reprefenting *Meander*, the famous River of Afia, who likewife had a great filver urne, and by him lay an Vnicorne.

In the midft of this border was fixed a rich Compartiment,

A 3   ment,

67 Inigo Jones (1573–1652)

Indamora, Queen of Narsinga

Pen and brown ink over gray wash
26.3 × 14.6 cm
Lent by the duke of Devonshire and the
Chatsworth Settlement Trustees

Indamora's headdress is probably based on that
of the Donzella Africana dell'Indie (African-
Indian girl) in Vecellio's *Habiti antichi et moderni*,
1598 (see p. 118 in Vaughan, "Salvages and Men
of Ind," above).

68   Inigo Jones (1573–1652)
      An Indian Shore
          Pen and brown ink, splashed with green and
          brown scene-painters' distemper
          23.2 × 33.1 cm
          Lent by the duke of Devonshire and the
          Chatsworth Settlement Trustees

Jones's scenery is closely patterned on Giulio Pa-
rigi's design for the setting of the Fleet of Amerigo
Vespucci, the fourth intermezzo in *Il Giudizio di
Paride* (1608), performed at the marriage of Cosimo de' Medici II. The inscription on Jones's
drawing reads, "3 Sceane/Sceane of an In/dian
shore and/a sea for the Qu/ens masq[ue] of In/
damora/1634."

"Whilst Yet Our World Was New, When not Discover'd by the Old"

Sir William Davenant, *The Cruelty of the Spaniards in Peru*, 1658

George Chapman and Sir William Davenant, the authors of two masques incorporating Indians, also wrote plays with references to, or settings in, the New World. Many of the themes were the same, and some emphasis was placed on gold and the wealth America offered. Davenant's *Cruelty of the Spaniards in Peru* dramatized Spanish greed and probably contributed to anti-Spanish sentiment in England. Chapman, Davenant, Shakespeare, and others mirrored English attitudes toward the Indians. Indians on stage were sometimes depicted as Noble Savages living in a world of beauty and innocence and at other times as the "wild and bruitish people, without Fayth . . . and with out any civilitie," as described by André Thevet in *The New Found Worlde*. The otherness of New World natives was portrayed with body paint and feathers and pagan sun worship. As the 17th century progressed, dramas depicting the English converting the Indians to Christianity or the conquest of Indians proclaimed England's destiny as a world power.

69   George Chapman (1559?–1634)

Eastward Hoe . . . Made by Geo: Chapman,
Ben: Jonson, Joh: Marston

London, for William Aspley, 1605
Shelf mark: STC 4971

Eastward Hoe provides a good sample of some English attitudes toward America and its people. Captain Seagull says to his companions, "Come boyes, *Virginia* longs till we share the rest of her Maidenhead." And, a short while later, "I tell thee, Golde is more plentifull there then Copper is with us. . . . Why man all their dripping Pans, and their Chamber pottes are pure Gold; . . . all the Prisoners they take, are fetterd in Gold: and for Rubies and Diamonds, they goe forth on holydayes and gather 'hem by the Sea-shore." Clearly the Indians do not share European attitudes toward precious metals and jewels. But, if they are lacking in civility, they are still a handsome people: "A whole Conntry of English is there man, bred of those that were left there in 79. They have married with the Indians and make 'hem bring forth as beautifull faces as any we have in England."

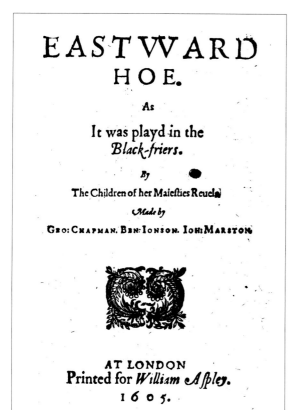

EASTWARD
HOE.

As

It was playd in the
Black-friers.

By

The Children of her Maiefties Reuela

Made by

Geo: Chapman. Ben: Ionson. Ioh: Marston

AT LONDON
Printed for *William Afpley.*
1 6 0 5.

Scap. But is there fuch treafure there Captaine, as I haue heard?
Sea. I tell thee, Golde is more plentifull there then Copper is with vs: and for as much redde Copper as I can bring, Ile haue thrice the waight in Golde. Why man all their dripping Pans, and their Chamber pottes are pure Gold;. and all the Chaines, with which they chaine vp their ftreetes, are maffie Golde; all the Prifoners they take, are fetterd in Gold: and for Rubies and Diamonds, they goe forth on holydayes and gather 'hem by the Sea-fhore, to hang on their childrens Coates, and fticke in their Capps, as commonly as our children weare Saffron guilt Brooches, and groates with hoales in 'hem.

70   Theodor de Bry (1528–1598)

Americae pars sexta. Sive Historiae ab Hieronymo Benzono

    [Frankfurt], 1596
    Shelf mark: G 159 B7 1590 v.2 Cage

Captain Seagull's belief that the New World was full of gold and other fabulous riches was shared by many. Everyone knew of the gold and silver flowing into Spain from Peru and Mexico, and many could remember stories of Francis Drake's successful voyage to Panama in 1572–1573 when he brought back gold, silver, and pearls. Surely Virginia was flowing with gold too. Engravings produced by the de Bry family must have added to the stories of the New World's riches. This one shows the Indians of Peru bringing their gold to Pizarro to ransom Athabalipa, their king.

The Scene, an vn-inhabited Island

Names of the Actors.

Alonso, K. of Naples:
Sebastian his Brother.
Prospero, the right Duke of Millaine.
Anthonio his brother, the vsurping Duke of Millaine.
Ferdinand, Son to the King of Naples.
Gonzalo, an honest old Councellor.
Adrian, & Francisco, Lords.
Caliban, a saluage and deformed slaue.
Trinculo, a Iester.
Stephano, a drunken Butler.
Master of a Ship.
Boate-Swaine.
Marriners.
Miranda, daughter to Prospero.
Ariell, an ayrie spirit.
Iris
Ceres
Iuno   } Spirits.
Nymphes
Reapers

71   William Shakespeare (1564–1616)
      The Tempest, in *Comedies, Histories & Tragedies*
         London, Isaac Jaggard and Ed. Blount,
         1623
         Shelf mark: STC 22273, no. 13

When Trinculo first encounters Caliban, he wonders whether Caliban is a man or a fish and then considers the fortune he might make if he could put Caliban on display in London. His pal Stephano agrees that "salvages and men of Ind" can be very profitable. It is not clear whether Shakespeare meant for Caliban to be a native of the New World. His name is an anagram of cannibal, and he is a dispossessed native of a "brave new world," but he is also the son of an Algerian witch. Whether a native of America or of some other new world, Caliban does seem to be an example of the "wild and bruitish people" described by Thevet. Shakespeare called him "a salvage and deformed slave." His struggles with the "civilizing" influences of the Europeans who land on his island are not unlike the experiences of Native Americans.

72 Sir William Davenant (1606–1668)
The Cruelty of the Spaniards in Peru: Exprest by Instrumentall and Vocall Musick

London, for Henry Herringman, 1658
Shelf mark: D 321

During the interregnum, under the Cromwells, theatrical extravaganzas disappeared from England. Under the guise of opera, however, William Davenant kept theater alive in London. Because England was at war with Spain, two main functions of Davenant's *Cruelty of the Spaniards in Peru* were to portray the Spanish as demons and to glorify the English. Perspective scenery represented the pastoral habitat of the Peruvians, "differing from those of *European* Climats by representing of *Coco-Trees*, *Pines* and *Palmitos*;

. . . *Munkies*, *Apes* and *Parrots*; and at farther distance Vallies of *Sugar-Canes*." Indian sun worship and feather apparel were featured.

The first song depicts the Indians' golden world, "E're crafty Cities made us tame" when "none were rich by bus'ness made." Then the natives knew no poverty; their nakedness provoked no shame, for "all were innocent." The remaining scenes of the drama include Spanish torment of the Indians, and the drama ends with the English and Indians shaking hands, although Davenant admits that "the English had made no discovery of Peru, in the time of the Spaniards first invasion there." (For a fuller discussion of the opera, see Vaughan, "Salvages and Men of Ind," above.)

The Cruelty of the

SPANIARDS

IN

PERU.

Exprest by Instrumentall and
Vocall Musick, and by Art of
Perspective in Scenes, &c.

Represented daily at the *Cockpit*
in *DRURY-LANE*,
At Three after noone
punctually.

LONDON,
Printed for *Henry Herringman*, and are to be sold at his Shop
at the *Anchor* in the Lower walk in the
New Exchange. 1658.

73 Theodor de Bry (1528–1598)
Americae pars sexta. Sive Historiae ab
Hieronymo Benzono
    [Frankfurt], 1596
    Shelf mark: G 159 B7 1590 v.2 Cage

Not only did engravings by the de Bry family serve to spread stories and images of New World gold and silver, they also depicted in graphic detail the cruel treatment of the Indians by the Spanish. The influence of the prints was so widespread that they may well have provided some inspiration for Davenant even though he was writing many years after the engravings were first issued. Girolamo Benzoni's *Historia del Mondo Nuovo* was one of the prin-

cipal works to spread the so-called Black Legend of Spanish cruelty. The de Brys published Urbain Chauveton's Latin translation of Benzoni in three parts between 1594 and 1596, with numerous engravings illustrating the text. This one illustrates the pillaging of Cuzco, Peru, by the Spanish in 1533, vividly showing the savage treatment of the Peruvians.

"Our Old World Modestly Withdrew and Here in Private, Had Brought Forth a New!"

John Dryden, *The Indian Emperour*, 1667

By the time of the Restoration of Charles II in 1660, much of the wonder generated by Indians on stage had disappeared. A number of plays still had New World settings, sometimes merely as an exotic background for traditional European plots, but sometimes also as propaganda against the Spanish and promoting English efforts in the New World. The Indians are often presented as having European values, and there are heroes and villains among both the Indians and the Europeans. The story of Montezuma was presented in *The Indian-Queen*, although the authors, Sir Robert Howard and John Dryden, took great liberties with history. It was such a success that Dryden produced a sequel entitled *The Indian Emperour*. He called Montezuma's story *"perhaps the greatest, which was ever represented in a Poem of this Nature; (the action of it including the Discovery and Conquest of a New World.)"*

The Indian-Queen.

ACT. V. SCEN. I.

The Scene opens, and discovers the Temple of the Sun all of Gold, and four Priests in habits of white, and red Feathers attending by a bloody Altar, as ready for sacrifice.

Then Enter the Guards, and Zempoalla, and Traxalla; Ynca, Orazia, and Montezuma bound; as soon as they are plac'd the Priest sings.

74   Sir Robert Howard (1626–1698) and
John Dryden (1631–1700)
The Indian-Queen, in *Four New Plays*
London, for Henry Herringman, 1665
Shelf mark: H 2995

The Indian-Queen is a heroic tragedy whose noble young protagonists, the Indians Montezuma and Acacis, become rivals in love. Written nearly 150 years after the events it purports to represent, the play takes incredible liberties with history. Montezuma, a general in the Peruvian army, serves the Peruvian king, yet later is revealed to be the lawful heir to the kingdom of Mexico. Spectacle is used to represent Indian culture. The usurping Mexican queen, Zempoalla, is decked with wreaths of feathers. After Montezuma has been captured, *"The Scene opens, and discovers the Temple of the Sun all of Gold, and four Priests in habits of white, and red Feathers attending by a bloody Altar, as ready for sacrifice."* The setting and culture are exotic and the "naked Indians" differ from Europeans in their "untaught" simplicity, but their emotional struggles are very European. (For a fuller discussion of this play, see Vaughan, "Salvages and Men of Ind," above).

FOUR NEW

PLAYS,

Viz:

The {S U R P R I S A L, {Comedies.
{C O M M I T T E E,

The {I N D I A N-Q U E E N, {Tragedies.
{V E S T A L-V I R G I N,

As they were Acted by His MAJESTIES
Servants at the *Theatre-Royal.*

Written by the Honourable
Sir *ROBERT HOWARD.*

IMPRIMATUR,

March 7.
166 4/7.   *Roger L'Estrange.*

LONDON,

Printed for *Henry Herringman*, and are to be
fold at his Shop at the *Blew-Anchor* in the Lower
Walk of the New-Exchange. 1665.

MUTECZUMA

Rex ultimus Mexicanorum

75   John Ogilby (1600–1676)

America

London, by the author, 1671

Shelf mark: O165

Ogilby's *America*, published just a few years after *The Indian-Queen* and its sequel, *The Indian Emperour*, includes a portrait of Montezuma that emphasizes his nobility and his position as king of Mexico. Like many other late 17th-century depictions of American Indians, however, this portrait presents its subject as dark-skinned.

THE
Indian Emperour,
OR,
THE CONQUEST OF
MEXICO
BY THE
SPANIARDS·

Being the Sequel of the *Indian Queen*.

By JOHN DRYDEN Efq;

The Second Edition.

Dum relego fcripfiffe pudet, quia plurima cerno
Me quoque, qui feci, judice, digna lini. Ovid.

LONDON,

Printed for *H. Herringman*, at the Sign of the *Blew Anchor* in the
Lower walk of the *New Exchange.* 1668. S

76   John Dryden (1631–1700)
The Indian Emperour
London, for H. Herringman, 1668
Shelf mark: D 2289 copy 1

Since *The Indian-Queen* had been such a success, Dryden followed it with a play using the same scenes and costumes and extending the plot to Montezuma's and Zempoalla's sons and daughters. Their heroic intrigues take place during Cortés's arrival and the subsequent destruction of Aztec civilization and the death of Montezuma. Dryden implies throughout the play that despite their sacrificial rites, the Indians' natural nobility is superior to European cruelty and corruption, a view he probably adapted from Montaigne. (See Vaughan, "Salvages and Men of Ind," above.)

Oroonoko :

A

TRAGEDY

As it is Acted at the

Theatre=Royal,

By His Majesty's Servants.

First Edition.

Written by *THO. SOUTHERNE.*

---- *Quo fata trahunt, virtus secura sequetur.* Lucan.

*Virtus recludens immeritis mori
Cœlum, negatâ tentat iter viâ.*
Hor. Od. 2. lib. 3.

L O N D O N :
Printed for *H. Playford* in the *Temple-Change. B. Tooke*
at the *Middle-Temple-Gate.* And *S. Buckley* at the
Dolphin against St. *Dunstan's* Church in *Fleetstreet.*
M DC XC VI.

---

77   Thomas Southerne (1660–1746)
  Oroonoko, a Tragedy
      London, for H. Playford, B. Tooke, and
      S. Buckley, 1696
      Shelf mark: S 4761

Southerne's tragedy is based on a novel by Aphra Behn. Indians play a fairly minor role, for the principal character is the black slave Oroonoko, a prince among his own people. The heroic treatment here is of the second stage in England's colonial enterprise—full settlement, the near-destruction of the Indians, and the importation of African slaves to work large plantations. Although Southerne inserted an Indian rebellion in the middle of his play, one that is quelled by Oroonoko, it is clear that the Indians have ceased to symbolize England's destiny and have become merely a theatrical backdrop.

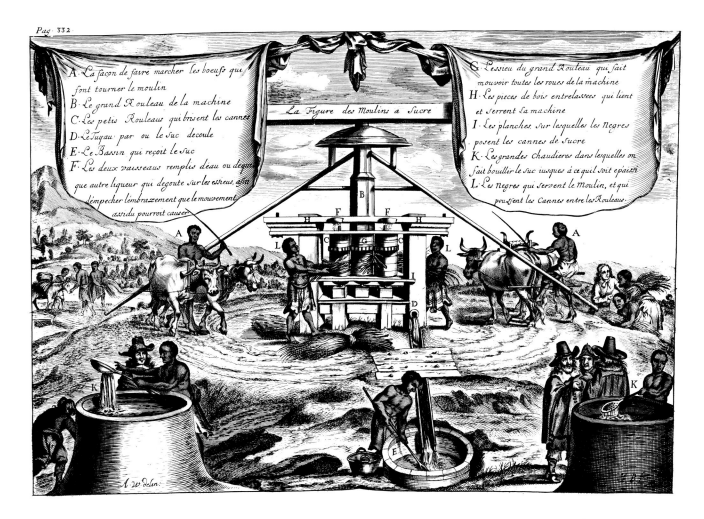

A. La façon de faire marcher les boeufs qui font tourner le moulin
B. Le grand Rouleau de la machine
C. Les petis Rouleaux qui brisent les cannes
D. Le Tuyau par ou le suc decoule
E. Le Bassin qui reçoit le suc
F. Les deux vaisseaus remplis d'eau ou de que autre liqueur qui degoute sur les essieus, afin d'empecher l'embrazement que le mouvement assidu pourroit causer

La Figure des Moulins a Sucre

G. L'essieu du grand Rouleau qui fait mouvoir toutes les roues de la machine
H. Les pieces de bois entrelassees qui lient et serrent la machine
I. Les planches sur lesquelles les Negres posent les cannes de Sucre
K. Les grandes chaudieres dans lesquelles on fait bouillir le suc iusques à ce qu'il soit epaissi
L. Les Negres qui servent le Moulin, et qui poussent les Cannes entre les Rouleaus.

78   Charles de Rochefort (b. 1605)
*Histoire Naturelle . . . des Iles Antilles de
l'Amerique*
Rotterdam, Arnout Leers, 1665
Shelf mark: F 2001 R6 1665 Cage

This engraving from Rochefort's history of the
Caribbean islands shows the use of African slaves
on a sugar plantation.

THE

Widdow Ranter

OR,

The HISTORY of

Bacon in Virginia.

A

TRAGICOMEDY,

Acted by their Majefties Servants.

Written by Mrs. A. Behn.

LONDON, Printed for *James Knapton* at the Crown in St. *Paul's* Church-Yard. 1690.

79 Aphra Behn (1640–1689)
The Widdow Ranter
    London, for James Knapton, 1690
    Shelf mark: B 1774

Aphra Behn, who had visited Suriname, presents in *The Widdow Ranter* a somewhat more realistic picture of English experience in the New World. Nathaniel Bacon had quelled two Indian uprisings in Virginia and then used his authority to confront the royal governor and capture Jamestown for a while in 1676. The play, while supporting Bacon and the English position, does ascribe responsibility for the Indians' situation to the English: "the *Indians* by our ill Management of Trade, whom we have Armed against Our selves, Very frequently make War upon us with our own Weapons."

Although he fights the Indians, in the play Bacon falls in love with the Indian queen Semernia, who implores him not to harm her people. But before Bacon can act, he is set upon by the governor's men and renounced as a traitor. Suspecting English treachery, the Indians prepare for war in a scene with Indian priests and priestesses dancing around an idol "*with ridiculous Postures and Crying (as for Incantations). Thrice repeated,* Agah Yerkin, Agah Boah, Sulen Tawarapah, Sulen Tawarapah." We can only speculate as to whether this scene resembles anything Aphra Behn saw in Suriname.

The Indian Queen

J. Smith ex.

W. Vincent fe.

80 William Vincent
    The Indian Queen
        Mezzotint, [c. 1700]
        Shelf mark: ac 232569

This mezzotint portrait is of the actress Anne Bracegirdle, the first to play the role of the Indian queen in *The Widdow Ranter*. Her costume is basically European, but she wears a feather headdress. She is attended by two very African-looking boys, who also wear feather headdresses; one of them wears a feather skirt.

The Golden Land

Visions of Paradise

Two different stories or sets of beliefs about the Garden of Eden existed during the late Middle Ages. According to one version, the garden had been destroyed by the Flood. According to the other, it had survived far from the inhabited world, cut off by mountains or seas that men could not cross. Numerous explorers thought they might find Eden in a remote land where the climate resembled a perpetual spring.

The natural abundance of the New World, its tropical flora, the gold ornaments worn by the Indians, and aspects of the native way of life led Columbus to believe that he had found the garden in the West Indies. Reports of property held in common, along with many drastic differences between the mentalities of the Old World and the New suggested to some Europeans that America was a land of liberty, equality, and peace, where people were "naturally" good. In spite of hardships encountered by early colonists and conflicts between them and the Native Americans, a predominant European image of the New World was of a land where life was easy, food was abundant, and a harmony existed between man and nature. In *The Decades of the Newe Worlde* (1555), Richard Eden said, "They seeme to lyve in the goulden worlde, without toyle, lyvinge in open gardens . . . without lawes, without bookes, and without Judges." In Davenant's opera *The Cruelty of the Spaniards in Peru* (1658), the Indians sing of their golden world "E're crafty Cities made us tame" when "none were rich by bus'ness made," when "all were innocent."

Another component of the growing myth about America, the golden land, was the belief that humans and animals lived together harmoniously in a nature that generously provided sustenance. Adding to the myth were stories of the Fountain of Youth and the city of El Dorado, paved with gold. Michael Drayton's poem "Virginia" (1606) described even this more northern land as one

Where Nature hath in store
Fowle, Venison and Fish,
And the Fruitfull'st Soyle
Without your Toyle
Three Harvests more,
All greater than your Wish.

The Dutch artist Jan van der Straet, in *Venationes Ferarum, Avium, Piscium* [1630?], depicted an idyllic setting where pelicanlike birds fished for the Indians.

Many elements of the title page to Willem Piso's *Historia Naturalis Brasiliae* (1648), suggest that the artist was depicting an American Adam and Eve surrounded by lush vegetation and numerous animals and sea life in an Edenic setting. Even the serpent is present, twined around the tree behind Adam.

In spite of the failure of the search for El Dorado, the image of America flowing with gold was a persistent one, supported by the great wealth that did flow into Spain from Mexico and South America. This image is summed up in a detail from the frontispiece to Arnoldus Montanus's, *De Nieuwe en Onbekende Weereld* (1671).

The vision of a virgin, and as yet unexploited, golden land gave rise very early to European expectations of easy-to-gain wealth from gold, silver, and natural resources. America was an overflowing cornucopia. "I tell thee, Golde is more plentifull there then Copper is with us. . . . and for Rubies and Diamonds, they goe forth on holydayes and gather 'hem by the Sea-shore," reported Captain Seagull in Chapman's *Eastward Hoe* (cat. no. 69).

Hardship and Profit

Although Columbus had not found a route to the East and its wealth, his voyages opened the way for European exploitation of the resources of the new world he did find. These events brought about dramatic changes for the natives of this "new golden land." Before long whole populations disappeared from the Caribbean islands, exterminated by diseases brought by the Europeans. Systematic enslavement of American natives under Spanish rule also effected partial depopulation on the southern continent. As commercial enterprise flourished, labor shortages led to the development of a slave trade, which eventually brought millions of Africans to America. European countries realized tremendous profits from commerce with the "West Indies," but for the colonists themselves, the land did not yield up its wealth without toil.

In spite of the highly developed Aztec civilization and the relatively small numbers of Spanish soldiers, the conquest of Mexico by the Spanish was a relatively easy one. Bartolomé de Las Casas's *Narratio*

The torture of Cuauhtemoc, one of the Aztec rulers who became a popular hero for resisting the conquistadors, is illustrated in the 1614 de Bry edition of Las Casas.

Regionum Indicarum publicized Spanish oppression and torture of the Indians, adding to the Black Legend of Spanish cruelty.

The Spanish were the first to produce sugar in the Caribbean and to export it. Its cultivation was soon developed in Mexico, Paraguay, and Peru, and by 1526 the Portuguese had begun shipping sugar from Brazil to Lisbon. Slave labor played a major role in the colonization of America because it permitted the large-scale harvesting of sugar, indigo, and tobacco, and the mining of precious metals, thus contributing greatly to the profits of European companies.

Before the decline of Dutch influence in the second half of the 17th century, Dutch companies concentrated their commercial efforts on the sugar plantations of northern Brazil, and on the Portuguese slave trade that furnished the necessary labor. The Dutch West India Company, established in 1621 to counter Spanish power in the New World, became a symbol of the enormous profit that could be derived from successful colonization and exploitation of New World territories.

During the 17th century, both France and England had developing colonies in the New World, and numerous publications in both countries promoted colonization. English authors described Virginia as a kind of heaven on earth and encouraged true English patriots to make their fortunes there. Edward Waterhouse's *A Declaration of the State of the Colony and Affaires in Virginia* (1622) presented a glorious description of "this spacious and fruitfull country of Virginia . . . naturally rich . . . abounding with as many natural blessings." However, it also set forth, over several pages, the names of the victims of

In *Les Indes Orientales et Occidentales et Autres Lieux* [1700?], the Dutch artist Romein de Hooghe depicted the production of sugar in Brazil.

giſſen/ ende is daer naer by eenighe noch achter-haelt: behalven dat in ſommi-
ghe kaſſen Silver al veel Gouts is ghevonden.

In 't Schip vande Generael, ghenaemt Amſterdam.
   Silver in kaſſen ende barren 24870½ pondt.
     57 Kaſſen Cochenille Miſteca.
   130 Hoo kaſſen als balen Cochenilla Silveſtre, ende Indigo Guatemalo.
    31 Pondt 10 oncen Gout.
   Een kaſken daer in ketens ende platen 6; pondt 8 oncen Gout.
   Een kaſken daer in twee ketens ſeven of acht pondt Gout.
   Seven pondt veerthien oncen Ambregris.
  1000 Peerlen.
    37 Pondt Muſcus.
    12 Pondt Bezoar Occidentael.
   Voorts vele kleynigheden van Gout ende Gheſteenten.

In 't Schip vanden Ammirael, den Hollandtſchen Thuyn.
   Silver in kaſſen ende barren 18953 pondt.
   Ghemaeckt Silver 130 pondt.
    16 Packen Cochenille Miſteca.
   319 Kaſſen Indigo ofte Cochenille Silveſtre.
   Een Kaſken met 1255 Realen van achten.
   Eenighe kaſſen met ghemaeckt Silver-werck.
   Eenighe met ghemaeckte Stoffen van Zijde.
   Ende veel andere koſtelijckheden.
  3592 Huyden uyt het Galeon.

In 't Schip Haerlem.
    37 Kaſſen Cochenille Miſteca.
   152 Kaſſen Indigo Guatemalo.
  2046 Stucx Weſt-Indiſche Huyden.

In 't Schip Gelderlandt.
   Silver in kaſſen weghende 6922 pondt.
     2 Balen Cochenille Miſteca.
    89 Kaſſen Indigo Guatemalo.
  2196 Stucx Weſt-Indiſche Huyden.
   622 Stucken Campeche-hout.

In 't Schip Hollandia.
   Silver in kaſſen ende barren 7397 pondt.
   Vier packen Cochenille Miſteca.
   126 Kaſſen Indigo Guatemalo.
  1999 Stucx Weſt-Indiſche Huyden.
    34 Stucx Campeche-hout.
     7 Yſere Stucken.

In 't Schip de Swarte Leeuwe.
   Silver in 43 kaſſen weghende 2864½ pondt.
    24 Kaſſen Cochenille Miſteca.
    68 Kaſſen Indigo Guatemalo.

In 't Schip de Roode Leeuwe.
    40 Balen Cochenille Miſteca.
    79 Kaſſen Indigo Guatemalo.

In 't Schip de Provincie van Uytrecht.
   Silver in kaſſen en barren weghende 10382 pondt.

                          T   18 Kaſ=

Accounts for the year 1628, from a history of the West India Company by Johannes de Laet (*Historie ofte Iaerlijck Verhael* [1644]), list some of the principal items transported by the company's ships, including cochineal, indigo from Guatemala, timber [Hout], pearls, silver, and so on.

THE INCONVENIENCIES

THAT HAVE HAPPENED TO SOME PERSONS WHICH HAVE TRANSPORTED THEMSELVES

from *England* to *Virginia*, vvithout prouisions necessary to sustaine themselues, hath greatly hindred the *Progresse* of that noble *Plantation*: For preuention of the like disorders heereafter, that no man suffer, either through ignorance or misinformation; it is thought requisite to publish this short declaration: wherein is contained a particular of such necessaries, as either priuate families or single persons shall haue cause to furnish themselues with, for their better support at their first landing in Virginia, whereby also greater numbers may receiue in part, directions how to prouide themselues.

Apparrell.

Apparrell for one man, and so after the rate for more.

	li.	s.	d.
One Monmouth Cap	00	01	10
Three falling bands		01	03
Three shirts		07	06
One waste-coate		02	02
One suite of Canuase		07	06
One suite of Frize		10	00
One suite of Cloth		15	00
Three paire of Irish stockins		04	—
Foure paire of shooes		08	08
One paire of garters		00	10
One doozen of points		00	03
One paire of Canuase sheets		08	00
Seuen ells of Canuase, to make a bed and boulster, to be filled in *Virginia* 8.s.		08	00
One Rug for a bed 8. s. which with the bed seruing for two men, halfe is			
Fiue ells coorse Canuase, to make a bed at Sea for two men, to be filled with straw, iiij.s.		05	00
One coorse Rug at Sea for two men, will cost vj.s. is for one			
	04	00	00

Victuall.

For a whole yeere for one man, and so for more after the rate.

	li.	s.	d.
Eight bushels of Meale	02	00	00
Two bushels of pease at 3.s.		06	00
Two bushels of Oatemeale 4.s. 6.d.		09	00
One gallon of *Aquauitæ*		02	06
One gallon of Oyle		03	06
Two gallons of Vineger 1. s.		02	00
	03	03	00

Armes.

For one man, but if halfe of your men haue armour it is sufficient so that all haue Peeces and swords.

	li.	s.	d.
One Armour compleat, light		17	00
One long Peece, fiue foot or fiue and a halfe, neere Musket bore	01	02	—
One sword		05	—
One belt		01	—
One bandaleere		01	06
Twenty pound of powder		18	00
Sixty pound of shot or lead, Pistoll and Goose shot		05	00
	03	09	06

Tooles.

For a family of 6. persons and so after the rate for more.

	li.	s.	d.
Fiue broad howes at 2.s. a piece		10	—
Fiue narrow howes at 16.d. a piece		06	08
Two broad Axes at 3.s. 8.d. a piece		07	04
Fiue felling Axes at 18.d. a piece		07	06
Two steele hand sawes at 16.d. a piece		02	08
Two two-hand-sawes at 5. s. a piece		10	—
One whip-saw, set and filed with box, file, and wrest		10	—
Two hammers 12.d. a piece		02	00
Three shouels 18.d. a piece		04	06
Two spades at 18.d. a piece		03	—
Two augers 6.d. a piece		01	00
Sixe chissels 6.d. a piece		03	00
Two percers stocked 4 d. a piece		00	08
Three gimlets 2.d. a piece		00	06
Two hatchets 21.d. a piece		03	06
Two froues to cleaue pale 18.d.		03	00
Two hand bills 20. a piece		03	04
One grindlestone 4.s.		04	00
Nailes of all sorts to the value of	02		
Two Pickaxes		03	—
	06	02	08

Houshold Implements.

For a family of 6. persons, and so for more or lesse after the rate.

	li.	s.	d.
One Iron Pot		07	—
One kettle		06	—
One large frying pan		02	06
One gridiron		01	06
Two skillets		05	—
One spit		02	—
Platters, dishes, spoones of wood		04	—
	01	08	00

	li.	s.	d.
For Suger, Spice, and fruit, and at Sea for 6.men	00	12	06
So the full charge of Apparrell, Victuall, Armes, Tooles, and houshold stuffe, and after this rate for each person, will amount vnto about the summe of	12	10	—
The passage of each man is	06	00	—
The fraight of these prouisions for a man, will bee about halfe a Tun, which is	01	10	—
So the whole charge will amount to about	20	00	00

Nets, hookes, lines, and a tent must be added, if the number of people be greater, as also some kine. And this is the vsuall proportion that the *Virginia Company* do bestow vpon their Tenants which they send.

Whosoeuer transports himselfe or any other at his owne charge vnto *Virginia*, shall for each person so transported before Midsummer 1625 haue to him and his heires for euer fifty Acres of Land vpon a first, and fifty Acres vpon a second diuision.

Imprinted at London by FELIX KYNGSTON. 1622.

As a practical matter, Waterhouse included a list of "provisions necessary to sustaine themselves" for prospective colonists.

the "barbarous massacre . . . treacherously executed by the Native Infidels upon the English" in 1622.

Waterhouse ends his pamphlet: "To conclude then, seeing that Virginia is most abundantly fruitfull, and that this Massacre must rather be beneficiall to the Plantation than impaire it, let all men take courage, and put to their helping hands, since now the time is most seasonable and advantagious for the reaping of those benefits which the Plantation hath long promised."

America: The Fourth Continent

For Europeans, America was indeed a "new world of wonders." The vast differences between Europe and America were emphasized in those objects and aspects of the new land that Europeans collected, displayed, studied, and illustrated and in the stereotyped images that came to represent America. Faced with so many novel, and often conflicting, images of a country and a way of life that were "altogether estrangfull," 16th- and 17th-century Europeans were unable to comprehend the complexity and variety of American cultures. Instead, they focused on a few of the most arresting and unusual aspects of America and its peoples, substituting symbols—nakedness, feathers, gold, cannibalism, bows and arrows, wooden clubs, and exotic flora and fauna—for real understanding.

Allegorical or emblematic depictions of America began to appear only in the second half of the 16th century. Although most Europeans knew that America was a separate continent, only gradually was the notion of a fourth continent reconciled with the traditional legend of the world's having been divided into three by the sons of Noah after the Flood. The three Magi often represented the three continents, but emblematic depictions of the continents did not develop until there were four of them. By the end of the 16th century, allegorical representations of Europe, Asia, Africa, and America could be found in the decorative borders of maps, on title pages (especially of atlases), on triumphal arches, and as participants in public festivities celebrating royal entries and marriages. They were usually, but not always, presented as women, probably because the mythological figure of Europa, who gave her name to Europe, was a woman. The symbolic attributes of the allegories emphasized their differences and set them apart from each other.

Opus nunc denuo ab ipso Auctore recognitum, multisque locis castigatum, & quamplurimis
nouis Tabulis atque Commentarijs auctum

81   Abraham Ortelius (1527–1598)
      Theatrum Orbis Terrarum
          Antwerp, Ex Officina Plantiniana, 1595
          Shelf mark: G1015 O6 1595 Cage

Probably the first allegorical depiction of America appeared on the title page to the 1570 edition of Ortelius's *Theatrum Orbis Terrarum*. America is one of four, or possibly five, continents, which also appear in this 1595 edition; they are described in introductory verses by Adolphus Merkerchus of Bruges. Europe is at the top; Asia and Africa appear on the left and right; and America lies at the bottom of the page. She is naked except for a helmetlike cap of feathers, similar to the one on van der Straet's America (cat. no. 3), and a leg band like that worn by Aldrovandi's Brazilian man

(cat. no. 42; leg bands were a detail on which numerous artists focused—see cat. nos. 13, 40, 58, 60, 64, and 84). A Tupinamba club is in her right hand (see cat. nos. 3, 47, 52, 54, and 55), and a severed head, representing cannibalism, is in the other. A bow and arrows lie at her feet.

Beside her, a bust of another woman, with flames in her breast, represents Magallanica. Merkerchus's verses indicate that only the head, or top part, of the land of Magallanica is known, so only the top part of the woman can be depicted. He also says that the people there light many fires: hence the flames. The reference must be to Tierra del Fuego, the archipelago south of the Strait of Magellan in southern South America.

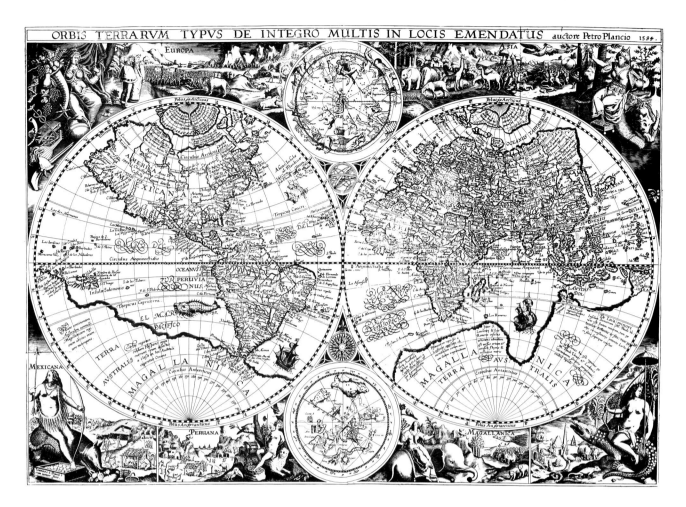

82   Jan Huygen van Linschoten (1563–1611)
      Navigatio ac Itinerarium
          The Hague, Albert Henricsz., 1599
          Shelf mark: ac 164285

The world map of Petrus Plancius (1552–1622), engraved by Jan van Doetecum (fl. 1559–1608), was separately issued in 1594 and incorporated into editions of Linschoten's *Itinerarium* beginning in 1599. The elaborate pictorial border represents Europe, Asia, Africa, Magallanica, and North and South America, as Mexico and Peru. Mexico appears as a woman, naked except for an animal skin slightly reminiscent of those in Harriot (cat. no. 20), with tattoos on her legs. She holds a bow and arrow and rides an armadillo. In the background can be seen dwellings and the surrounding landscape; in the foreground fish and salamanders are being dried over a fire. Fruits and vegetables,

including corn and squash, are at the woman's feet, along with a box of what may be pearls. Peru, also a nearly naked woman, wears a feather headdress, carries a long-handled anchor axe (see cat. no. 51), and rides a leopard. Nearby are a toucan, a parrot, a monkey, and other animals. In the background are Indian dwellings and a scene of cannibalism. Like Mexico's, her feet rest on a container of what may be pearls. The large southern continent of Magallanica (Antarctica) incorporates Tierra del Fuego, but the pictorial representation of Magallanica in the border associates it more closely with Asia or Africa than with the New World.

83　Willem Janszoon Blaeu (1571–1638)
Appendix Theatri A. Ortelii et Atlantis G. Mercatoris

Amsterdam, Willem Blaeu, 1631
Shelf mark: G 1015 B5 1631 Cage

The representation of America on this title page is unusual. While the continents of Europe, Asia, and Africa are symbolized by women, America appears as a man. He wears a feather headdress and a feather skirt and carries some type of club. The reason for representing America as a man is not clear, nor is the significance of the figures seated directly above the continents. The Blaeu firm used this title page border in several atlases. Part of the inspiration for it may be found in a world map by Claes Janszoon Visscher issued in Amsterdam about 1617. The top panel of Visscher's map portrays a fashionably dressed Europe flanked by natives of the other continents, Asia, Africa, Magallanica, Mexicana, and Peruviana. Here Peru is presented as a man riding on an armadillo, and his attire is almost identical to that of the Indian man on Blaeu's title page. The sex of Mexicana is difficult to determine but may be male, as is that of Africa. Even when America (Mexico and Peru) is represented as a man, his dress and attributes are much the same as those of America when depicted as a woman.

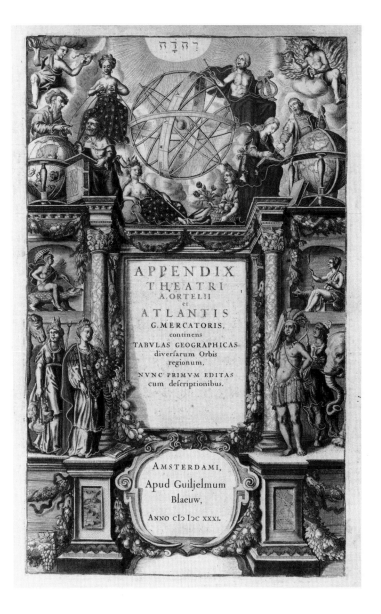

AMERICA

T' AMSTERDAM
By Jacob van Meurs, *Plaetsnijder en Boeckverkooper op de Keysers graft in de Stadt Meurs. 1671*

84   Arnoldus Montanus (1625?–1683)
      De Nieuwe en Onbekende Weereld
         Amsterdam, Jacob Meurs, 1671
         Shelf mark: E 143 M7 1671 Cage

The engraved title page to Montanus's book on the New World sums up much of the imagery that had come to be associated with America by the late 17th century. The wealth of America is symbolized by the central figure, who holds a cornucopia with one hand while she throws down gold and jewels with the other. Gold is also visible in the head and body ornaments worn by some of the other Indians in the engraving. Feather headdresses, capes, and skirts are much in evidence. Many of the natives are shown only partially clothed, to make the viewer aware of the nakedness characteristic of inhabitants in the New World. Although most of the Indians have dark skin, two in the foreground do not. A few are armed with spears and clubs. The artist seems to have intentionally represented the variety to be found in the dress, ornaments, and features of different New World peoples. New World animals and products are also shown. In the background are armed Europeans, ships, and a stone fort with cannons. Montanus's *America*, therefore, is a scene of conquest in which America gives up her wealth to the conquerors, one of whom has his arms spread wide to receive it.

Bibliography

Altick, Richard D. *The Shows of London*. Cambridge: Belknap Press of Harvard University Press, 1978.

Anderson, Frank J. *An Illustrated History of the Herbals*. New York: Columbia University Press, 1977.

Arents, George. *Books, Manuscripts, and Drawings Relating to Tobacco from the Collection of George Arents, Jr*. Exh. cat. Washington, D.C.: U.S. Government Printing Office, 1938.

Baudet, Henri. *Paradise on Earth: Some Thoughts on European Images of Non-European Man*. New Haven: Yale University Press, 1965.

Bibliothèque Sainte-Geneviève. *Le Cabinet de curiosités . . . des origines à nos jours*. [By Françoise Zehnacker and Nicolas Petit.] Paris: Bibliothèque Sainte-Geneviève, 1989.

Blumenthal, Arthur R. *Theater Art of the Medici*. Hanover, N.H.: Dartmouth College Museum and Galleries, 1980.

Boxer, C. R. *Race Relations in the Portuguese Colonial Empire, 1415–1825*. Oxford: Clarendon Press, 1963.

Brandon, William. *New Worlds for Old: Reports from the New World and Their Effect on the Development of Social Thought in Europe, 1500–1800*. Athens: Ohio University Press, 1986.

Braudel, Fernand. *The Structures of Everyday Life: Civilization & Capitalism, 15th–18th Century*. New York: Harper & Row, 1981. 3 vols.

Broc, Numa. *La Géographie de la Renaissance (1420–1620)*. Paris: Bibliothèque Nationale, 1980.

Bucher, Bernadette. *Icon and Conquest: A Structural Analysis of the Illustrations of de Bry's Great Voyages*. Chicago: University of Chicago Press, 1981.

Bush-Brown, Louise. *Men with Green Pens: Lives of the Great Writers on Plants in Early Times*. Philadelphia: Dorrance, 1964.

Camporesi, Piero. *Il Brodo indiano*. Milan: Garzante Editore, 1990.

Cawley, Robert R. *The Voyagers and Elizabethan Drama*. Boston: Modern Language Association of America, 1938.

Columbus, Christopher. *The Journal*. Trans. Cecil Jane. London: The Hakluyt Society, 1960.

———. *The Letter of Columbus on the Discovery of America*. Translation and reprint of the oldest four editions in Latin. New York: Trustees of the Lenox Library, 1892.

Crosby, Alfred W. *The Columbian Exchange: Biological and Cultural Consequences of 1492*. Westport, Conn.: Greenwood Publishing Co., 1972.

Cumming, W. P., R. A. Skelton, and D. B. Quinn. *The Discovery of North America*. London: Elek, 1971.

Duchet, Michèle. *L'Amérique de Théodore de Bry. Une Collection de voyages protestante du XVIe siècle*. Paris: Editions du CNRS, 1987.

Duviols, Jean-Paul. *L'Amérique espagnole vue et rêvée. Les Livres de voyages de Christophe Colomb à Bougainville*. Paris: Promodis, 1985.

Elliott, J. H. *The Old World and the New, 1492–1650*. Cambridge: Cambridge University Press, 1970.

Emerson, Edward R. *Beverages, Past and Present: An Historical Sketch*. New York: G. P. Putnam's Sons, 1908. 2 vols.

L'Entrée de Henri II à Rouen, 1550. Facsimile ed. Introduction by Margaret M. McGowan. Amsterdam: Theatrum Orbis Terrarum, [n.d.].

Feest, Christian F. "The Virginia Indian in Pictures, 1612–1624." *Smithsonian Journal of History* 2:1 (1967), pp. 1–20.

———. "Virginia Indian Miscellany III." *Archiv für Völkerkunde* 26 (1972), pp. 1–14.

Festivities, Ceremonies, and Celebrations in Western Europe, 1500–1790. Exh. cat. Providence: Brown University, 1979.

First Images of America: The Impact of the New World on the Old. Ed. Fredi Chiappelli. Berkeley: University of California Press, 1976. 2 vols.

Franklin, Alfred. *Le Café, le thé, & le chocolat.* Paris: E. Plon, Nourrit et Cie, 1893.

Gerbi, Antonello. *Nature in the New World: From Christopher Columbus to Gonzalo Fernández de Oviedo.* Pittsburgh: University of Pittsburgh Press, 1985.

Góngora, Mario. *Studies in the Colonial History of Spanish America.* Cambridge: Cambridge University Press, 1975.

Greenblatt, Stephen. *Marvelous Possessions: The Wonder of the New World.* Oxford: Clarendon Press, 1991.

Greene, Edward Lee. *Landmarks of Botanical History.* Stanford: Stanford University Press, 1983. 2 vols.

Heikamp, Detlef. *Mexico and the Medici.* Florence: Editrice Edam, 1972.

Hodgen, Margaret T. *Early Anthropology in the Sixteenth and Seventeenth Centuries.* Philadelphia: University of Pennsylvania Press, 1964.

Honour, Hugh. *The New Golden Land: European Images of America from the Discoveries to the Present Time.* New York: Pantheon Books, 1975.

Hulme, Peter. *Colonial Encounters: Europe and the Native Caribbean, 1492–1797.* London: Methuen, 1986.

Hulton, Paul, and David Beers Quinn. *The American Drawings of John White, 1577–1590, with Drawings of European and Oriental Subjects.* London: Trustees of the British Museum, 1964.

Jacquot, Jean. *Les Fêtes de la Renaissance.* Paris: Editions du CNRS, 1956–1975. 3 vols.

Laurencich-Minelli, Laura. "Oggetti americani studiati da Ulisse Aldrovandi." *Archivio per l'Antropologia e la Etnologia* 113 (1983), pp. 187–206.

Laurencich-Minelli, Laura, and Alessandra Filipetti. "Per le collezioni americaniste del Museo Cospiano e dell'Istituto delle Scienze. Alcuni oggetti ritrovati a Bologna." *Archivio per l'Antropologia e la Etnologia* 113 (1983), pp. 207–225.

Lestringant, Frank. *Le Huguenot et le Sauvage. L'Amérique et la controverse coloniale en France au temps des guerres de religion.* Paris: Aux Amateurs de Livres, 1990.

Levin, Harry. *The Myth of the Golden Age in the Renaissance.* Bloomington: Indiana University Press, 1969.

Ley, Willy. *Dawn of Zoology.* Englewood Cliffs, N.J.: Prentice-Hall, 1968.

Lillywhite, Bryant. *London Coffeehouses.* London: Allen and Unwin, 1963.

Locy, William A. *The Growth of Biology.* London: G. Bell & Sons, Ltd., 1925.

Lowood, Henry. "The New World and Natural History." Paper presented at conference, America in European Consciousness, John Carter Brown Library, Providence, R.I., June 5–9, 1991.

Maltby, William S. *The Black Legend in England: The Development of Anti-Spanish Sentiment, 1558–1660.* Durham, N.C.: Duke University Press, 1971.

Martin, John Rupert. *The Decorations for the Pompa Introitus Ferdinandi.* London: Phaidon, 1972.

Mayor, A. Hyatt. *Prints & People: A Social History of Printed Pictures.* New York: Metropolitan Museum of Art, 1971.

Morison, Samuel Eliot. *The European Discovery of America.* New York: Oxford University Press, 1971–1974. 2 vols.